Using Excel

for beginners

Linda Steven

WHSMITH LTD, SWINDON, WILTS. SN3 3LD
in association with:

PEARSON EDUCATION LIMITED
Head Office:
Edinburgh Gate, Harlow, Essex CM20 2JE
Tel: +44 (0)1279 623623 Fax: +44 (0)1279 431059

London Office:
128 Long Acre, London WC2E 9AN
Tel: +44 (0)20 7447 2000 Fax: +44 (0)20 7240 5771
Website: www.it-minds.com

First published in Great Britain 2001
© Pearson Education Limited 2001

British Library Cataloguing in Publication Data
A CIP catalogue record for this book can be obtained from the British Library.

ISBN 0-130-65277-6

10 9 8 7 6 5 4 3 2 1

Typeset by Pantek Arts Ltd, Maidstone, Kent.
Printed and bound in Great Britain by Ashford Colour Press, Gosport, Hampshire.

The publishers' policy is to use paper manufactured from sustainable forests.

contents

introduction

Excel 2000 is a spreadsheet program that helps you work with numbers, calculations and forecasts. You can use Excel to create simple lists or to import data from giant databases. You can then use the program to generate charts, graphs and even maps to illustrate your financial reports.

There are icons throughout the book and these indicate notes that will give you more detail on certain points or explain new ideas. Each icon tells you what type of information the note provides (see below).

+info *These notes provide additional information.*

 These notes warn you of potential pitfalls, and explain how to avoid them.

 These notes list shortcuts, advanced techniques, etc.

If you've not used Excel 2000 before then it's best to read the chapters in order, starting with the basics, e.g. how to install the Excel 2000 program and how to call up an 'Office Assistant' icon (whose role it is to answer any queries you have). If you're familiar with Excel then simply jump straight to the chapter you're interested in.

I

Discovering the software

- **Installing Excel 2000**
- **Starting Excel 2000**
- **Discovering the screen**
- **Worksheets**
- **Cells**
- **Dialogue boxes**
- **Getting to know the Office Assistants**

Installing Excel 2000

To be able to install and use Excel 2000, you will need:

- a 486 or Pentium PC;
- Windows 95 or later, or Windows NT (Windows 2000 is recommended);
- a minimum RAM of 8 MB;
- a hard disk with approximately 100 MB free disk space for a complete installation;
- a CD-ROM reader;

- a Windows-compatible screen;
- a Microsoft-compatible mouse.

To install Excel 2000:

1 Switch on your computer and start Windows.
2 Insert the CD-ROM called 'Excel 2000' or 'Office 2000' into your drive.
3 Click the **Install** button.
4 Follow the instructions that appear on the screen.

Starting Excel 2000

To start Excel 2000:

1 Click the **Start** button in the Taskbar.
2 Select **Programs**.
3 Click on **Microsoft Excel** (Fig. 1.1).

Excel should now be launched, and the default worksheet 1 of workbook 1 displayed (Fig.1.2).

Figure 1.1

Starting Excel 2000.

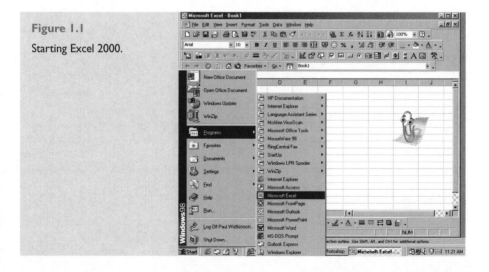

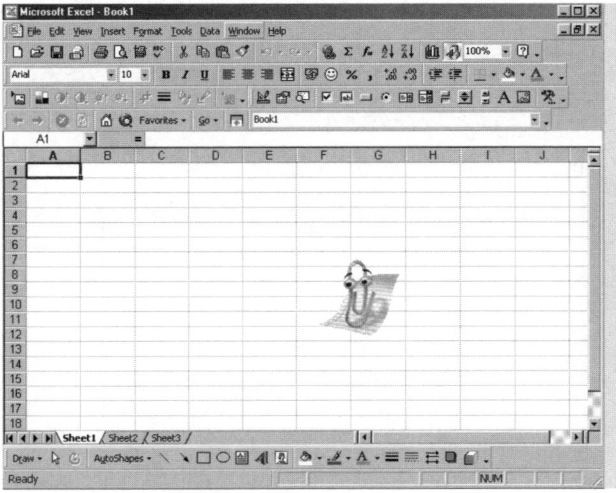

Figure 1.2

Worksheet 1 of workbook 1 is displayed as the default.

Discovering the screen

Before you start working, you need to discover the Excel screen, and then customise it. Excel is a nifty piece of software, if you take the trouble to get to know it properly.

The Excel window

In the top right-hand corner of the screen, there is a button called Restore Window (Fig. 1.3). This allows you to toggle between full-screen display and a display in a window.

If you click on this, the worksheet will be displayed in a window (Fig. 1.4).

The Maximize icon will bring the display back to full screen.

The black cross icon, located next to the Maximize and Restore Window icons, closes the window.

The Title bar

This is located at the top of the window. It indicates the name of the application, 'Microsoft Excel'.

3

Figure 1.3

The Restore Window button.

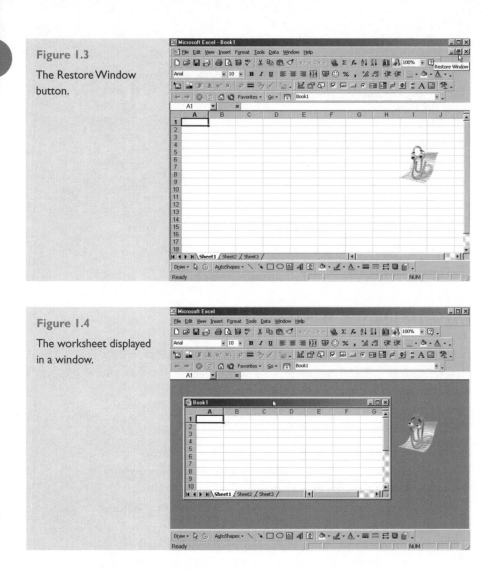

Figure 1.4

The worksheet displayed in a window.

The Menu bar

This is located under the Title bar. It lists the names of the nine drop-down menus (Fig. 1.5).

Figure 1.5

The Menu bar.

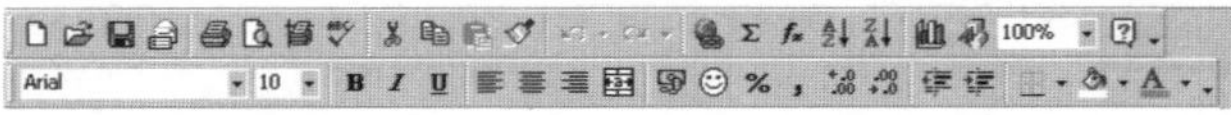

Arial   ▼ 10 ▼   **B** *I* <u>U</u>

Figure 1.6

The Standard and Layout toolbars.

The Toolbars

Excel offers nine default toolbars. You can customise existing toolbars and create new ones.

Two default toolbars are displayed: Standard and Layout (Fig. 1.6). To hide or display a toolbar, with the right-hand mouse button:

1 Click any toolbar.

2 In the context menu displayed, click the toolbar you wish to display or hide.

The Status bar

This is located at the bottom of the screen. The left side provides information about the mode you are working in. The right side shows whether keys such as Caps Lock are activated. To hide or display the Status bar, click **View**, **Status Bar**.

The Formula bar

This lets you view and modify the contents of the cells in your worksheet (Fig. 1.7). It shows the data you are entering into the cell. When it is active, the Cancel and Enter icons are displayed.

The name box

The name box, located under the toolbar, and to the left, indicates the active cell.

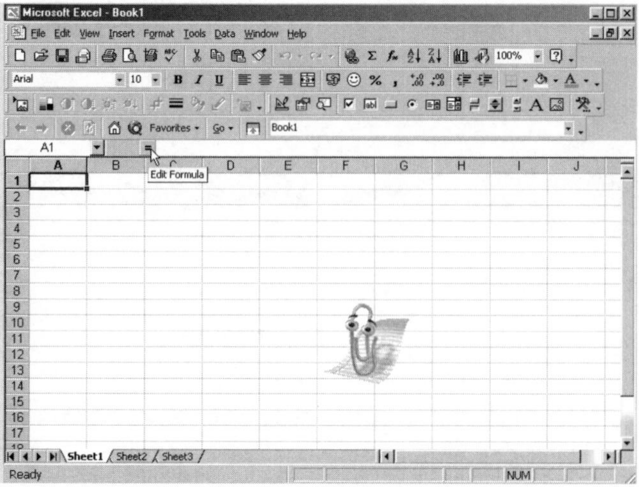

Figure 1.7

The formula bar.

ScreenTips

If you position the cursor on a button for a few seconds, but do not click the mouse, the function of the button will be explained in a ScreenTip. To deactivate ScreenTips:

1 Open the **View** menu.

2 Select **Toolbars**.

3 Choose **Customize**.

4 Click on the **Options** tab.

5 Untick the **Show ScreenTips on toolbars** box.

Scroll bars

The scroll bars and the scrolling arrows allow you to move quickly to view other sections in the worksheet.

To scroll through a column or a row, click the arrow in the vertical or horizontal scroll bar that points to where you wish to scroll.

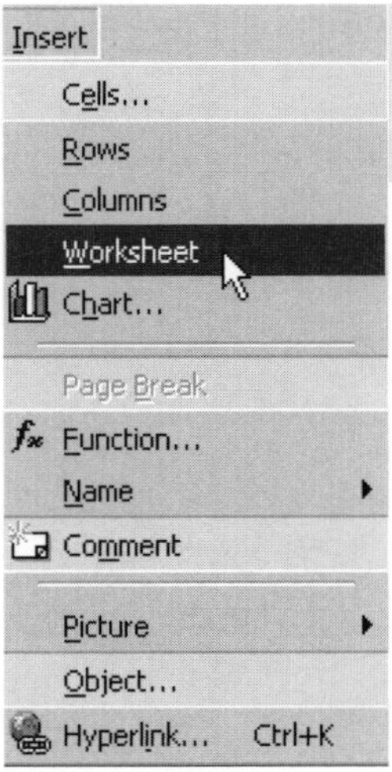

Insert

Cells...
Rows
Columns
Worksheet
📊 Chart...
Page Break
f Function...
Name ▶
📋 Comment
Picture ▶
Object...
🔗 Hyperlink... Ctrl+K

Figure 1.8

Adding a new worksheet.

Worksheets

A worksheet contains over 4 million cells arranged on 256 columns and 65 536 rows. A worksheet is stored in a workbook. The screen will only show you a small part of your worksheet.

A workbook includes several worksheets. Excel currently has three default worksheets, but you can add more whenever you wish. To add a worksheet:

1 Open the **Insert** menu.

2 Click the **Worksheet** option (Fig. 1.8).

To display the worksheet of your choice, select its tab.

Moving within the worksheet

To move between cells on the worksheet, use the following keys:

● **Up arrow**: move one cell up.

● **Down arrow**: move one cell down.

● **Left arrow**: move one cell left.

● **Right arrow**: move one cell right.

● **Home**: move to the first cell in the active row.

● **Page up**: move up one screen.

● **Page down**: move down one screen.

● **Ctrl+Page Down**: move to the next sheet in the workbook.

● **Ctrl+Page Up**: move to the previous sheet in the workbook.

- **Ctrl+Right arrow**: move to the next cell to the right that is not empty, or to the last cell in the row.
- **Ctrl+Left arrow**: move to the next cell to the left that is not empty, or to the first cell in the row.
- **Ctrl+Down arrow**: move to the next cell down that is not empty, or to the first cell in the column.
- **Ctrl+Up arrow**: move to the next cell up that is not empty, or to the first cell in the column.
- **Ctrl+Home**: move to the first cell in the worksheet (usually cell A1).
- **Ctrl+End**: move to the last cell in the worksheet, i.e. the cell at the intersection of the furthest right used column and the bottom-most used row.

Cells

The intersection of a row and a column is a cell. The cell is the primary element in Excel.

The active cell is surrounded by a thicker border. This is the cell that will be affected by your next action.

Each cell has its own address, which corresponds to the combination of the row number and the column letter.

To get into a cell, simply position the cursor on the cell you wish to make active and click.

Dialogue boxes

Dialogue boxes provide guidance and information as you work. They often include several pages; to access a particular page, click on its tab. A dialogue box may contain:

- **Text boxes.** To be filled with text typed in on the keyboard.
- **Option buttons.** Contain additional orders for executing a command. They are activated or deactivated with a single click.

- **Selection boxes.** The active selection is marked with a black circle.

- **Click-on list boxes.** Contain a list of predefined possibilities, one of which is selected by default.

- **Buttons.** Used to confirm or cancel your command. Some boxes also have extra buttons that allow you to open additional dialogue boxes.

- **Meters.** Small boxes with arrows pointing up and down to allocate numerical values.

- **Close box.** An icon in the shape of a cross, located in the top right-hand corner of the dialogue box. If you click this, the dialogue box will be closed.

Getting to know the Office Assistants

Excel 2000 provides you with eight assistants whose task it is to guide you through the application. The Office Assistant is an interactive program.

Each assistant answers questions on how to carry out specific tasks. To call them up, click the box with a question mark in the toolbar.

In the dialogue box that opens, type in a question.

For example, if you type in 'Office Assistant' and click the **Search** button, a character known as Clippit will ask you if you want to show, hide or turn off the Office Assistant, get help without using the Assistant, turn the Assistant sound on or off, see more, and so on.

If you click on **Options**, the Gallery and Options tabs are displayed. The Options tab offers various options that can be selected. The Gallery tab will introduce you to all the various Office Assistants.

2
Entering data

Opening a new workbook

When you launch Excel, it opens a new default workbook called 'Book 1'. You can work in this workbook and give it a name later.

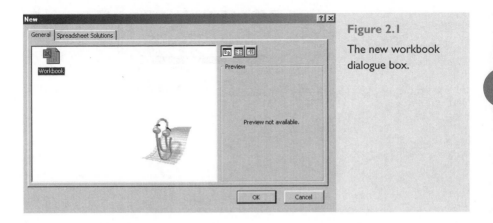

Figure 2.1

The new workbook
dialogue box.

To create a new workbook, open the **File** menu and select **New**. In
the **General** tab, click **Workbook**, then **OK** (Fig. 2.1).

The workbook that appears has three default worksheets. The
first one is the active worksheet.

Renaming the active worksheet

To rename the active worksheet, click with the right mouse button
on the tab of the active worksheet at the bottom left of the screen.
In the menu that is displayed, click **Rename**. The cursor is placed on
the tab to be renamed. Now just type in the new name.

Alternatively, while in the worksheet you want to rename, click on
Format, **Sheet**, **Rename** (Fig. 2.2). This will place the cursor on
the tab to be renamed. Type in the new name.

Opening an existing workbook

To open an existing workbook, select **File**, **Open**, and click on the
workbook in the dialogue box that is displayed.

Figure 2.2

Renaming the active
worksheet.

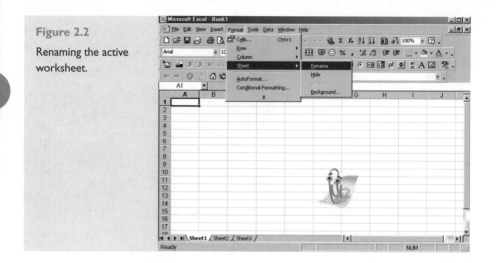

Entering data

To enter data, put the cursor in the cell you are interested in, then
click. This selects the cell. Now you can enter your data.

In Excel, anything that is not a number, date, time or formula is
text. Text can include figures, letters or symbols. It cannot exceed 32
000 characters per cell.

Using the currency style

To enter prices in an Excel worksheet, you can enter them as
whole numbers, or as currency with or without decimal points for
larger figures.

To access these different styles:

1 Open the **Format** menu.

2 Select **Cells**.

3 Choose the **Number** tab.

4 Select **Currency** in the **Category** list.

The currency styles are used for general currency values. If you wish to align decimal points, use the **Accounting** style in the **Category** list.

Modifying column width

As you type in text, you may see text in one column spilling over into the next. You therefore need to adjust the width of your columns.

Place the cursor on the boundary between two columns in the column headings (A, B, C, etc.) row. When the pointer becomes a bidirectional arrow click and drag the mouse until the column is the required width.

To adjust the column width automatically to its contents, double-click the border at the top right of the column.

Undo and Redo

With the keyboard

If you make a mistake, hold down the **Ctrl** key and then press **Z** (**Ctrl+Z**). This undoes your last action. If you use the same key combination again, you will undo the previous action, and so on up to 16 times. To redo an undo action, use the combination **Ctrl+Y**.

With the mouse

To undo an action using the mouse, click the **Undo** icon in the toolbar. If you click the black arrow to the right of this icon, a pull-down list lets you select the particular action to undo.

The **Redo** icon reverses an undo action. If you cannot see this icon on your toolbar, click on the **More Buttons** icon at the end of the Standard toolbar. This should then show the Redo icon.

Selecting cells

To select a single cell, just put the cursor in it and click.

To select a range of adjacent cells, click in the first cell of the range and then drag to the last cell.

To select a range of non-adjacent cells, select the first cell or range of cells, then hold down **Ctrl** and select the other cells or ranges.

To select a whole row or column, click the row or column heading.

To select the whole sheet, click the Select All button (the button between the first column and first row headings), or press **Ctrl+A**.

Finding and replacing

To find and replace the contents of several cells:

1 Select the range of cells in which you wish to make a replacement.

2 Open the **Edit** menu, then click **Replace**.

3 In the **Find what** field, type in the text or numbers you wish to replace.

4 In the **Replace with** field, type in the text or numbers that you wish to replace the previous entry with.

5 Then either click **Find Next**, and press **Replace** for each occurrence of the text that you want to replace; or click **Replace All** to replace everything in one go.

Clearing cells

To delete the contents of a cell or range:

1 Select the cell or range you wish to clear.

2 Open the **Edit** menu, and click **Clear** (Fig. 2.3).

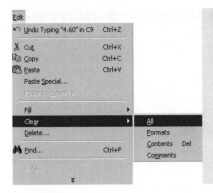

Figure 2.3

Clearing the contents of a cell.

3 Select **All** to clear the cell contents and remove all formatting; **Formats** to remove any formatting (e.g. bold) but leave the contents intact; **Contents** to delete the contents but leave any formatting; and **Comments** to remove any comments attached to the cells, but leave the contents and formatting.

Saving your work

When you have been working on your workbook for a while, you should save it to your hard disk:

1 Open the **File** menu, and select **Save**; or click on the **Save** button in the toolbar, which looks like a diskette.
2 Since you have not yet named your workbook, Book1 is the default title. In the dialogue box that appears, give your workbook a name in the **File name** box (Fig. 2.4).
3 Choose the folder to save it in and click **Save**.

To change the name of your workbook, or to save it to another drive:

1 Open the **File** menu.
2 Select **Save As**.
3 In the dialogue box that appears, select the drive where you wish to save your workbook.

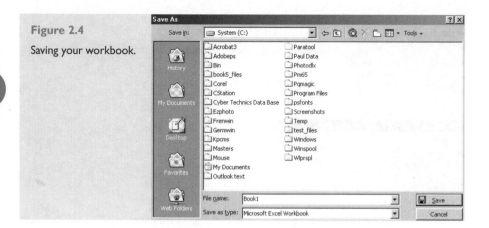

Figure 2.4

Saving your workbook.

4 In the **File name** field, enter the new name.

5 Click on **Save**.

Once your workbook has been named and saved, you only need to click the **Save** button to save any further changes.

Saving a workbook with its properties

To save a workbook with its properties:

1 Open the **File** menu.

2 Select **Properties**.

3 Click the **Summary** tab (Fig. 2.5).

4 Fill in the text boxes **Title**, **Subject**, and so on.

5 Add any necessary comments in the **Comments** box.

6 Confirm with **OK**.

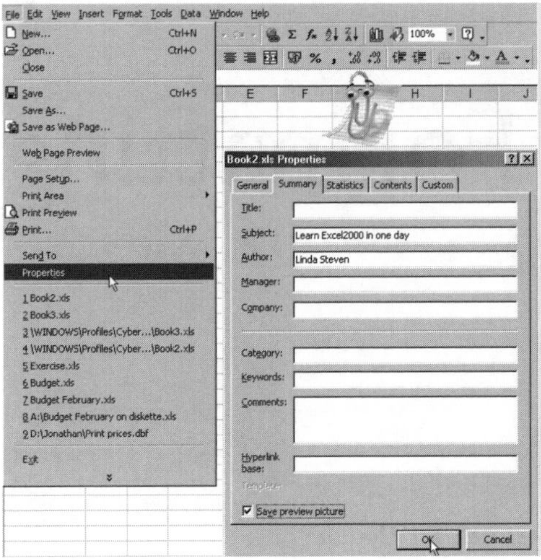

Figure 2.5

Saving properties for your workbook.

2 : Entering data

3
Formatting

- **Drag and drop**
- **Giving your worksheet a title**
- **Changing font and size**
- **Modifying a row height**
- **Modifying a column width**
- **Orienting text**
- **Adding a border**
- **Adding a pattern**
- **Automatic formatting**

Drag and drop

Before looking at the tools available in Excel to format your work area, you should learn how to move one or more cells with the drag and drop method.

1 Select the cell or range that you want to move.

2 Move the cursor over the edge of the selected area until it becomes an arrow.

3 Press and hold the mouse button, and drag the cells to a new position.

4 Release the mouse button when the cells are in the right place.

Giving your worksheet a title

To give your worksheet a name, type in the title in a cell at the top of the sheet. You will see that your title is left-aligned by default. To change the alignment of your title, select the cell and click on one of the following toolbar buttons.

● **Align Left**. Aligns text to the left of the cell.

● **Align Right**. Aligns text to the right of the cell.

● **Center**. Centres text within the cell.

To centre a title over several columns, select the columns across which you wish to centre your title (Fig. 3.1). Then click on the **Merge and Center** button in the toolbar.

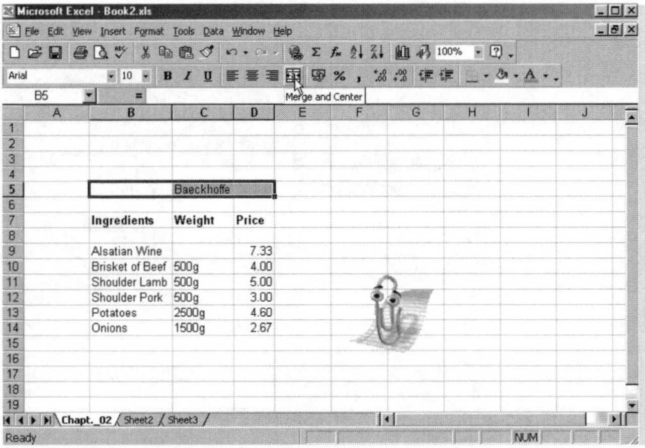

Figure 3.1

Centring a title over several columns.

Changing font and size

Changing the font

To use a different font:

1 Select the cells that you want to change the font in.

2 Open the **Format** menu.

3 Click on **Cells**.

4 Select the **Font** tab.

5 Choose the font you want to use from the **Font** list, then click **OK** (Fig. 3.2).

Changing the font size

To change the size of your characters:

1 Select the cells that you want to alter.

2 Open the **Format** menu.

3 Select **Cells**.

4 Click the **Font** tab.

5 Choose the size in the **Size** list, then click **OK**.

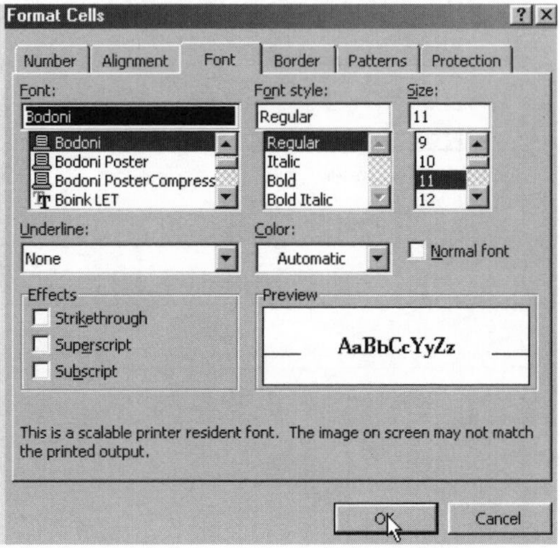

Figure 3.2

Changing the font.

Modifying a row height

There are two techniques you can use to change the height of a row.

Using the mouse

1 Select the row that you want to change the height of.

2 In the numbered row headings on the left-hand side of the page, position the cursor on the bottom border of the selected row. The cursor will change into a black arrow pointing up and down.

3 Press the mouse button, and move the cursor down until the row is the correct height.

4 Release the mouse button.

Using the Format menu

1 Select the row to be changed.

2 Open the **Format** menu.

3 Select **Row**.

4 Click on **Height**.

5 In the dialogue box, enter the exact height you want your row to be (Fig. 3.3).

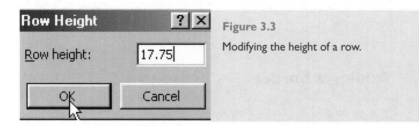

Figure 3.3

Modifying the height of a row.

Modifying a column width

To change the width of a column:

1 Select the column.

2 In the column headings at the top of the page, position the cursor on the right-hand border of the selected column. The cursor will change into a black arrow pointing left and right.

3 Press the mouse button, and move the cursor left or right until the column is the correct width.

4 Release the mouse button.

Orienting text

Inside a cell, text can be rotated by up to 90° clockwise or anti-clockwise.

1 Select the cell that contains the text to be rotated.

2 Open the **Format** menu.

3 Click on **Cells**.

4 Select the **Alignment** tab (Fig. 3.4).

5 In the **Orientation** section, select the number of degrees you wish to rotate your text through.

You may have to change the cell height for the rotated title to fit in properly.

Adding a border

To add a border to a range of cells:

1 Select the range.

2 Click the arrow next to the **Borders** toolbar button.

3 Click the type of border you require (Fig. 3.5).

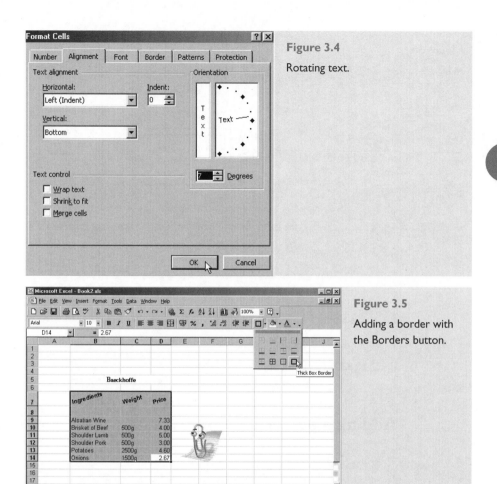

Figure 3.4

Rotating text.

Figure 3.5

Adding a border with the Borders button.

Alternatively, you can create a customised border:

1 Select the cells you want to apply a border to.

2 Open the **Format** menu.

3 Select **Cells**.

4 Click the **Border** tab (Fig. 3.6).

5 In the **Border** section, click on the icons corresponding to the parts of the cells you want to add a border to (top, left, etc.).

Figure 3.6

Adding a border using the menu.

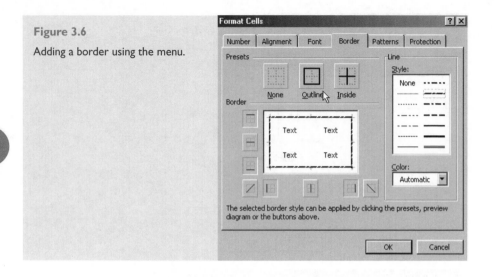

6 In the **Style** section, click on the type of border you would like.

7 In the **Color** section, select the colour.

8 Click **OK** to confirm.

Adding a pattern

To add a background pattern to a cell or range:

1 Select the cells.

2 Open the **Format** menu.

3 Select **Cells**.

4 Click the **Patterns** tab.

5 Click the arrow in the **Patterns** box.

6 Select the pattern that you want (Fig. 3.7).

7 Choose a colour by clicking on it.

8 Click **OK**.

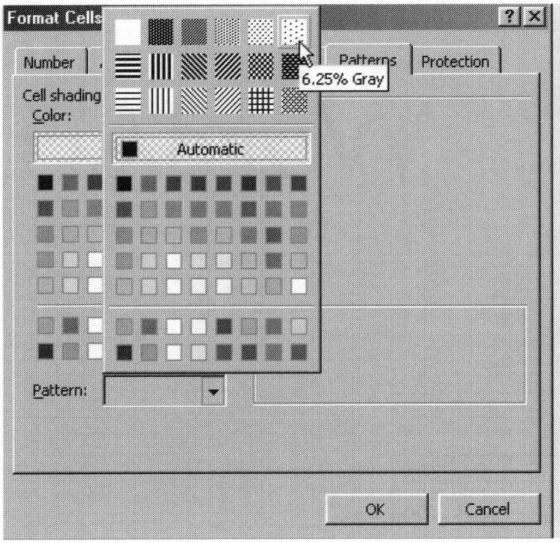

Figure 3.7
Selecting a pattern.

Adding background patterns to your worksheet

If you have a picture or pattern saved on your computer you can use it as a background to your worksheet.

1 Open the **Format** menu.

2 Click on **Sheet**.

3 Select **Background**.

4 Select the picture files you want to use for the background pattern. The selected picture is then reproduced over the whole worksheet.

Automatic formatting

Excel contains a number of predefined formats that you can apply to your worksheets. To use AutoFormat:

1 Open the **Format** menu.

2 Click on **AutoFormat**.

3 Choose one of the layouts offered.

4 Click **OK**.

4

WordArt

WordArt lets you add graphics to your Excel worksheets to improve their presentation.

Drawing graphic objects

The AutoShapes tool located in the Drawing toolbar contains 100 predefined shapes. First, open the Drawing toolbar.

1 Select the **View** menu.

2 Click on **Toolbars**.

3 Click on the **Drawing** button.

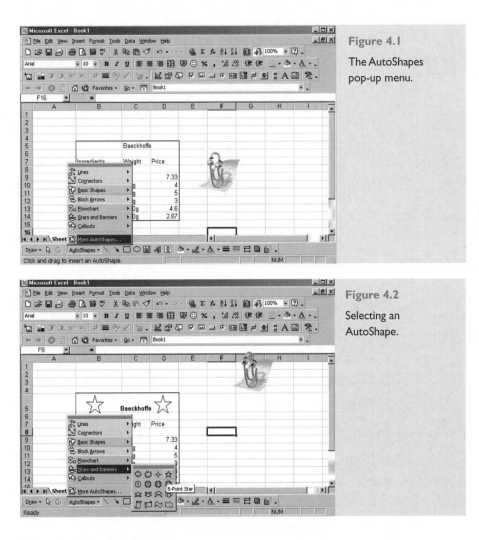

Figure 4.1

The AutoShapes
pop-up menu.

Figure 4.2

Selecting an
AutoShape.

To insert an AutoShape:

1 Click on the **AutoShapes** button (Fig. 4.1).

2 Choose the type of shape you want (Lines, Callouts, etc.).

3 Click on the shape you want to insert (Fig. 4.2).

4 Position your cursor where you want to insert the shape.

5 Holding down the mouse button, drag the cursor until the shape
  is the right size.

Figure 4.3

Adding colour to your AutoShape.

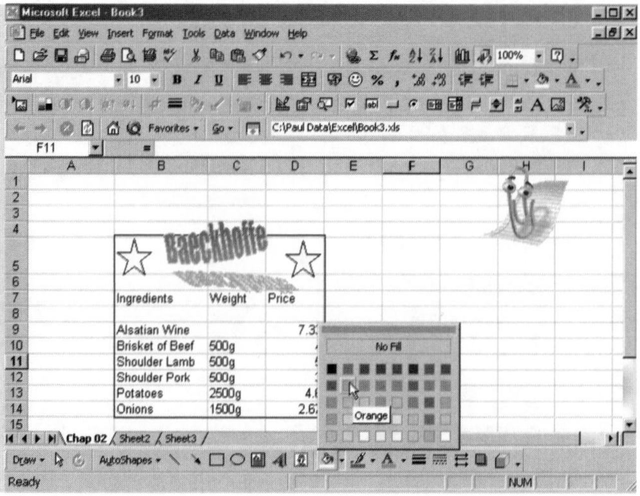

Adding colour

To add colour to your AutoShape:

1 Select the AutoShape by clicking in it.

2 Click the arrow on the **Fill Color** icon on the Drawing toolbar.

3 Click on the colour you want to use (Fig. 4.3).

To add colour to the outline of your AutoShape:

1 Select the AutoShape.

2 Click on the arrow in the **Line Color** button in the Drawing toolbar.

3 Click on the colour you want to use.

Adding text to an AutoShape

Once you have inserted your AutoShape, you can write inside it, unless it is a line, connector or freeform.

1 Select your AutoShape.

2 Position the cursor in the AutoShape, and type in your text.

Importing charts and pictures

If you have created a chart or picture in another application, you can copy and paste it into an Excel worksheet.

1 Click **Insert**.

2 Select **Picture**.

3 Click on **From File**.

4 Select your graphics file and click **Insert**.

You can insert ClipArt in a similar way.

Inserting a WordArt object

WordArt lets you add 3D effects to lines, AutoShapes and freeform objects. You can change the depth of a drawing, as well as its colour, angle, direction of light and the reflection on its surface.
First you must open the WordArt toolbar:

1 Click on **View**.

2 Select **Toolbars**.

3 Click on **WordArt**.

To create a title using WordArt effects:

1 Select the cell where you want to insert the title.

2 In the WordArt toolbar, click on the **Insert WordArt** button.

3 Click on the WordArt effect you want to use (Fig. 4.4).

4 Click **OK**.

5 Type your title into the dialogue box.

6 Change the font and size to suit your worksheet.

7 Click **OK**.

Figure 4.4

Enhance your title with a default WordArt effect.

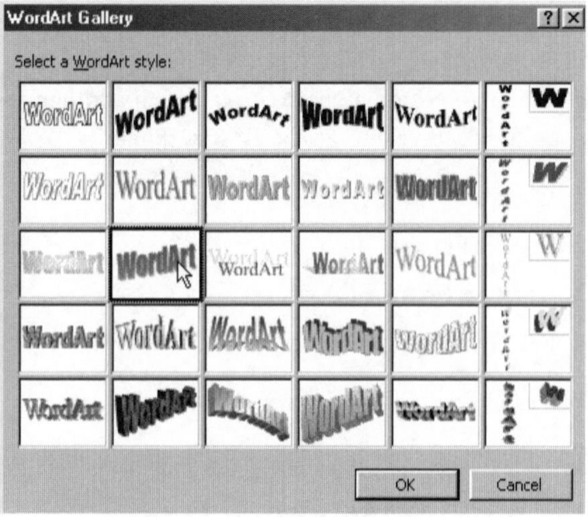

Rotating your title

To rotate your title:

1 Select the title by clicking in it anywhere.

2 Click the **Free Rotate** button in the WordArt toolbar. The pointer now changes to a black circular arrow.

3 Place the cursor over one of the green dots ('handles') surrounding the title.

4 Hold down the mouse button and drag the title until it is at the correct angle.

The ABC button

The WordArt Shape option represented by the ABC button lets you change the aspect of your WordArt title:

1 Select the title.

2 Click on **WordArt Shape**.

3 Click on the aspect you want to give your title (Fig. 4.5).

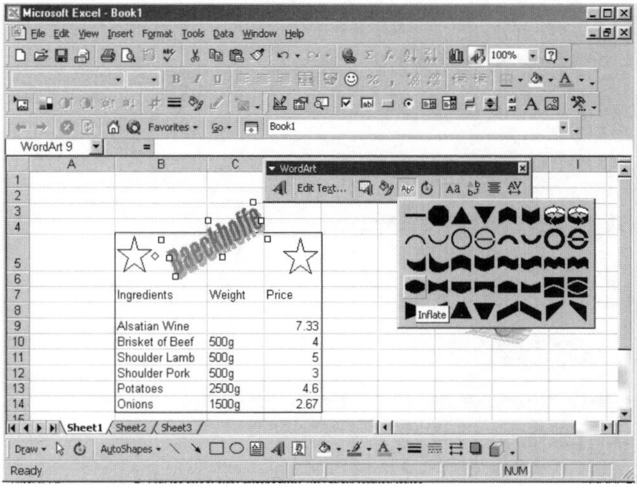

Figure 4.5

Selecting the Inflate
Bottom shape in
WordArt.

The Same Letter Heights button

This assigns the same height to all the letters in the selected WordArt object.

The Vertical Text button

This puts the letters in the selected WordArt object one on top of the other.

Using ClipArt

ClipArt is an internal image library of illustrations. It is useful if you do not have any of your own illustrations for your worksheets, but remember that all Excel 2000 users have the same library of ClipArt, so use in moderation!

To add some ClipArt:

1 Open the **Insert** menu.

2 Select **Picture**.

3 Click **ClipArt**.

31

4 Select an appropriate theme.

5 Click on the picture you want to use.

6 Click the **Insert clip** command button.

Adjusting lighting effects

To change the lighting effects in a title:

1 Select the title.

2 Click the **3-D** button in the Drawing toolbar.

3 Click **3-D Settings**.

4 Select the **Lighting** button (Fig. 4.6).

5 To adjust the direction of the light, click on the appropriate button.

6 To change the intensity of the light, click on **Bright**, **Normal** or **Dim.**

Figure 4.6

Choosing a lighting option.

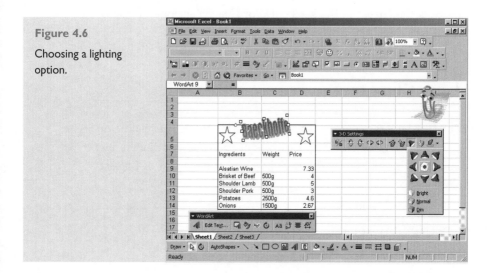

Modifying a 3D effect

To modify the 3-D effects of a title:

1 Select the title.

2 Click the **3-D** button in the Drawing toolbar.

3 Select **3-D Settings**.

4 Click on the appropriate buttons depending on the effects you wish to achieve.

● **3-D On/Off.** Applies a 3D format to the selected object using the default 3D choices, or cancels the 3D effect.

● **Tilt Down.** Tilts the 3D effect down by 6° on a horizontal axis. To tilt it up to 45°, hold down the **Shift** key and click the **Tilt Down** button.

● **Tilt Up.** Tilts the 3D effect up by 6° on a horizontal axis. To tilt it up to 45°, hold down the **Shift** key and click the **Tilt Up** button.

● **Tilt Right.** Tilts the 3D effect by 6° to the right on a vertical axis. To tilt it up to 45°, hold down the **Shift** key and click the **Tilt Right** button.

● **Tilt left.** Tilts the 3D effect by 6° to the left on a vertical axis. To tilt it up to 45°, hold down the **Shift** key and click the **Tilt Left** button.

● **Depth.** Adjusts the depth of a shape in 3D by 0 points to infinity (Fig. 4.7). A custom option allows you to define the number of points.

● **Direction.** Adjusts the perspective you wish to give to your object.

● **Lighting.** Adjusts the brightness for your object from nine different angles.

● **Surface.** Adjusts the way the surface of your object looks.

● **3D Color (Automatic).** Defines the colour you want to give your object.

Figure 4.7

Adding an 'Infinity' depth effect.

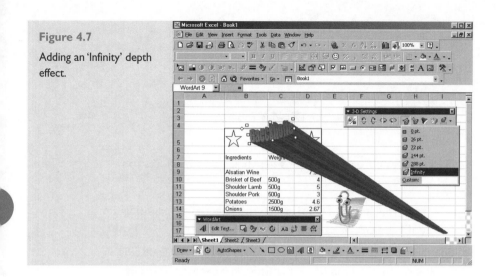

Adding a shadow

To add a shadow to a shape:

1 Select the shape

2 Click on the **Shadow** button in the Drawing toolbar.

3 Click on the type of shadow you want to add (Fig. 4.8).

> Shadow and 3D formatting are mutually exclusive. If you activate the shadow format, all 3D settings will be automatically deactivated, and vice versa.

To change the shadow effects:

1 After applying the shadow, reselect the shape:

2 Click on the **Shadow** button.

3 Select **Shadow Settings**.

4 Click on the relevant buttons.

● **Nudge Shadow Up**. Moves the shadow up incrementally.

● **Nudge Shadow Down**. Moves the shadow down incrementally.

● **Nudge Shadow Left**. Moves the shadow to the left incrementally.

● **Nudge Shadow Right**. Moves the shadow to the right incrementally.

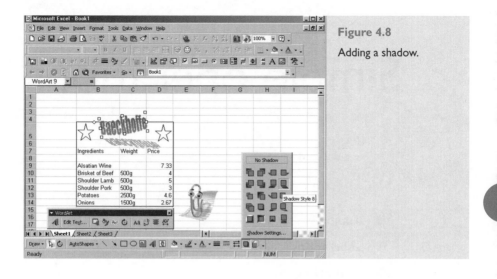

Figure 4.8

Adding a shadow.

5

Simple operations

- Adding
- Subtracting
- Multiplying
- Dividing
- Creating a formula
- Copying a formula
- Calculating an average

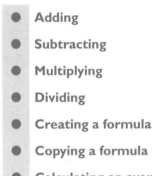 The main reason for using Excel 2000 is to carry out calculations.

Adding

For the following calculation examples, we will use the table shown in Fig. 5.1.

To calculate the total for a column of figures:

1 Click in the cell where you want the total to appear.

2 Type =. This tells Excel that you are creating a formula.

3 Click in the cell containing the first number to be added (in our example cell B9). The cell will be surrounded by flashing dotted lines, and the cell reference number will appear in the Formula bar.

Figure 5.1

Executing an addition operation with Excel 2000.

4 Now type +.

5 Click in the next cell to be added (in our case B10), then type in +. Repeat this until you get to the last cell (B12).

> Do not forget to enter the = sign before entering the formula, otherwise, Excel will not know that you are carrying out a calculation.

6 Confirm by pressing the **Enter** key. Your total is now displayed in the total cell (B14).

The AutoSum button

Another way of reaching this total is to use the AutoSum button in the Standard toolbar:

1 Click in the cell where you want the total to go (B14).

2 Click the **AutoSum** button (Fig. 5.2). The cell range included in the addition is automatically displayed in the Formula bar and in the total cell.

3 Confirm by pressing the **Enter** key. Your total is automatically displayed in the total cell.

Figure 5.2

Executing an additional
operation with the
AutoSum button.

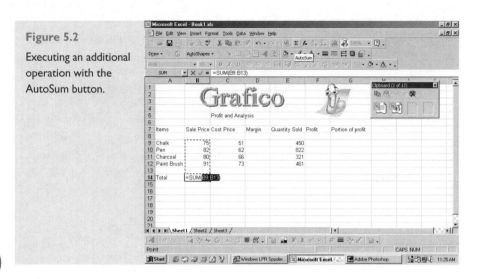

Subtotals

If your worksheet contains several subtotals generated from the Sum function, you can arrive at a grand total of the values using the AutoSum function. Click the cell where you want the grand total to go, select the **AutoSum** button, select the subtotals to be added, and press **Return**.

> When using the AutoSum function, if the range displayed is not the one you need, select the correct range in the normal way and press **Enter**.

Calculation operators

The addition sign is one of a number of 'operators'. Operators indicate the type of calculation to be performed.

Excel provides four different types of calculation operators (Table 5.1).

Table 5.1 Calculation operators available in Excel.

Arithmetic operators

+	Addition	
-	Subtraction/negative values	
*	Multiplication	
/	Division	
%	Per cent	
^	Exponential functions	

Comparison operators

=	Equal to	
>	Greater than	
<	Less than	
>=	Greater than or equal to	
<=	Less than or equal to	
<>	Not equal to	

Text operator

&	Links together two values to produce one continuous text value.

Reference operators

:	Range operator that produces one reference to all the cells between two references, including the two references.
,	Union operator that combines multiple references into one reference.

Subtracting

To calculate a subtraction:

1 Click in the cell where you want the subtraction total to appear.

2 Type in =.

3 Click in the first cell of the calculation.

4 Type in the - (minus) sign.

5 Click the second cell of the subtraction sum.

6 Press **Enter**.

Multiplying

To multiply cells:

1 Click in the cell where you want the product to appear.

2 Type in =.

3 Click in the first cell of the calculation.

4 Type in the * sign.

5 Click in the next cell of the calculation.

6 Press **Enter**.

Dividing

To perform a division calculation:

1 Click the cell where you want the calculation total to appear.

2 Type in the = sign.

3 Click the first cell of the calculation.

4 Type in the / sign.

5 Click the next cell of the calculation.

6 Press **Enter**.

Creating a formula

Formulas calculate values by following a specific order. All Excel 2000 formulas start with the = sign.

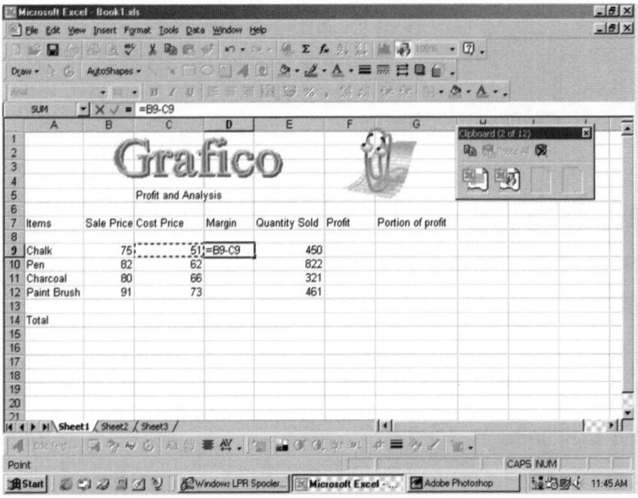

Figure 5.3

Calculating a margin
with Excel.

In our example worksheet, the 'Margin' column is the result of a
calculation relating to the 'Sale Price' and 'Cost Price' columns:

Margin = Sale price - Purchase price

To generate this formula for the first item (chalk) (Fig. 5.3).

1 Click in the cell in which you wish to display the formula (D9).

2 Type in the = sign.

3 Click in the cell that contains the first part of the formula (B9).

4 Type in the operator (-).

5 Click in the cell that contains the next part of the formula (C9).

6 Press **Enter** to confirm the calculation.

Copying a formula

If you *move* a formula, the cell references in the formula do not change.
When you *copy* a formula, the formula does not change but the cell
references do, so the copied formula will apply to different cells.

41

Using the same exapmle sheet as before, you can copy the formula from cell D9 to calculate the margins on the sale of the other items. There are three methods for doing this:

Method 1

1 Select the cell containing the formula to be copied (D9).

2 Open the **Edit** menu.

3 Select **Copy**.

4 Click in the cell(s) where you want to copy the formula to (D10:D12).

5 Open the **Edit** menu.

6 Select **Paste**.

7 Press **Enter**.

Method 2

1 Select the cell containing the formula to be copied (D9).

2 Position the cursor on the fill handle (bottom right) of the cell until the cursor becomes a small black cross.

3 Hold the left mouse button down and drag the fill handle until you have selected all the cells you want to copy the formula into (D10:D12).

4 Release the mouse button.

Method 3

1 Select the cell containing the formula to be copied (D9).

2 Click the **Copy** button in the toolbar.

3 Click in the cell(s) where you want to copy the formula to (D10:D12).

4 Press **Enter**.

Relative references

In all three of these methods, Excel copies the basic formula in cell D9.

When you copy it, the references in the initial formula are automatically adjusted.

Once you have copied the D1 formula into the other cells, click in turn on cells D10, D11 and D12. Look in the formula bar and you will see the formula changes slightly from B10-C10 to B11-C11 to B12-C12.

Each formula is always referenced to the two preceding cells on the same row.

Excel has simply added to each reference for the initial formula a number of rows corresponding to the position of the copy relating to the original formula.

Absolute references

A cell is an absolute reference when its address does not depend on the position of the formula, but is defined absolutely by its row and column references on your worksheet.

Going back to the same example, we can calculate the 'profit' column values as follows:

Profit = Margin * Quantity sold

To calculate the profit:

1 Select the cell where you wish to display the formula (F9).
2 Type in the formula (=D9*E9), and press **Return**.
3 Select the cell containing the formula (F9), and use the fill handle to copy the formula to the other cells (F10:F12).

The profit is automatically displayed in cells F10, F11 and F12.
The calculation formula for the 'Portion of profit' column is:

Portion of profit = Profit/Article/Total profit

1 First calculate the total profit (F14).
2 Type in the formula (=F9/F14).
3 Once you have obtained the value (0.269), click on the **Percent Style** button in the toolbar. The value is converted to a percentage.
4 Copy the formula for the three other articles. The error value #DIV/0! will be displayed in the cells (Fig. 5.4).

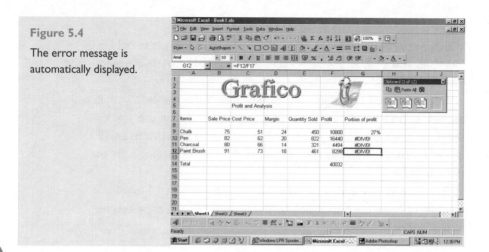

Figure 5.4

The error message is automatically displayed.

Go to each of these cells, and look at the Formula bar. The formula is modified every time. For example, cell G11 tells us that the formula is F11 divided by F16. F16 is an empty cell, and the value of an empty cell is zero by default, so Excel tells you that you are trying to divide by zero.

Instead of entering the relative formula for each cell, you can modify the initial (G9) formula so that the reference to the total profit (F14) does not change when it is copied. Rather than typing in the cell reference (F14), type in the absolute value (40032).

Calculating an average

To calculate the average margin for our example:

1 Select the cell where you want the average to appear.

2 Type in =Average.

3 Open a bracket.

4 Select the range you want to calculate the average for (D9:D12) (Fig. 5.5).

5 Close bracket.

6 Confirm by pressing the **Enter** key.

You can also use the Function Wizard to calculate an average.

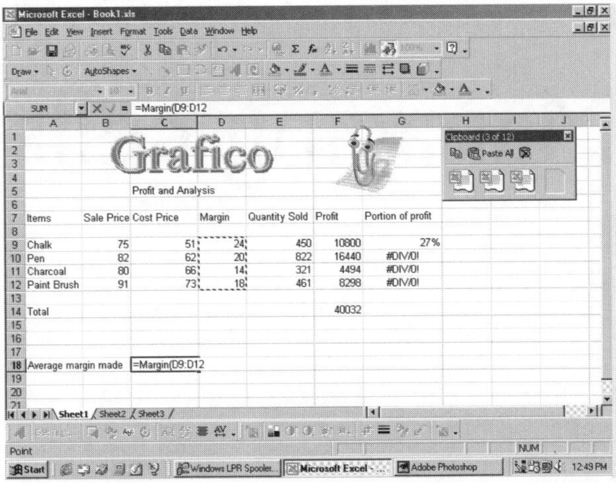

Figure 5.5

Calculating an average.

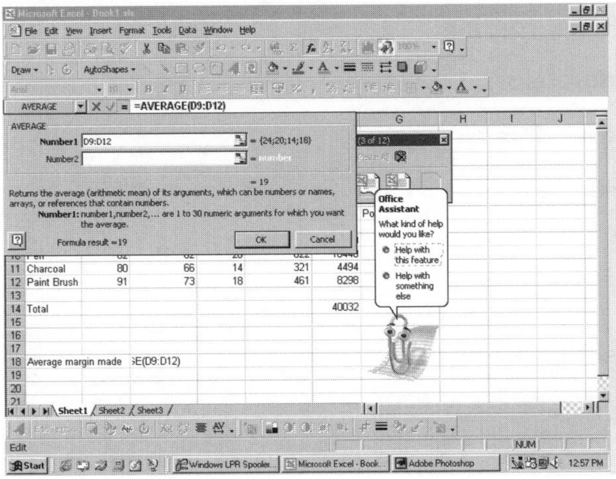

Figure 5.6

Calculating an average with the Function Wizard.

1 Select the **Paste Function** (f_x) icon in the toolbar.

2 Double click the **AVERAGE** option in the function name area.

3 In the Number 1 box, select the range for which you wish to calculate the average (Fig. 5.6).

4 Click **OK**.

> When you calculate an average, empty cells, and cells containing text or logical values, are not taken into account. Cells containg the value zero are taken into account.

6

Managing cells

- Moving cells
- Copying cells
- Incremental copying
- Protecting cells
- Naming a cell range
- Displaying data
- Searching for data
- Replacing data
- The spell checker
- Sorting data

Moving cells

Using the Clipboard

1 Select the range of cells to be moved.

2 Open the **Edit** menu.

3 Click **Cut**.

4 Place the cursor on the destination cell(s).

5 Open the **Edit** menu and click **Paste**.

Using the mouse

1 Select the cells to be moved.

2 Move the cursor over the cell range boundary until it becomes an arrow.

3 Press the left mouse button and drag the cells to their new position.

Copying cells

Using the Clipboard

1 Select the cells to be copied.

2 Open the **Edit** menu.

3 Click on **Copy**.

4 Select the destination cell(s).

5 Open the **Edit** menu.

6 Click on **Paste**.

> By default, Excel transfers all the attributes of the source cells. If you wish to copy specific attributes, use the Paste Special option, instead of Paste, and select the attributes you wish to copy.

Using the mouse

1 Select the cells to be copied.

2 Move the cursor over the cell range boundary until it becomes an arrow.

3 Hold down the **Ctrl** key, press the left mouse button and drag the cells to where you want to copy them.

Incremental copying

An incremental series is a series of words or numbers with a logical sequence, e.g. 1, 2, 3, 4, 5 or Monday, Tuesday, Wednesday.

You can automatically fill several types of series in Excel.

1 To specify the type of series, define the starting value for the series, e.g. 'Monday'.

2 Select the cell.

3 Click on the fill handle and drag down or across to complete your series.

Defining a customised list

You can define your own series for future use:

1 Open the **Tools** menu.

2 Select **Options**.

3 Click the **Custom Lists** tab (Fig. 6.1).

4 Type the new list into the **List entries** box.

5 Click **Add**.

6 Click **OK**.

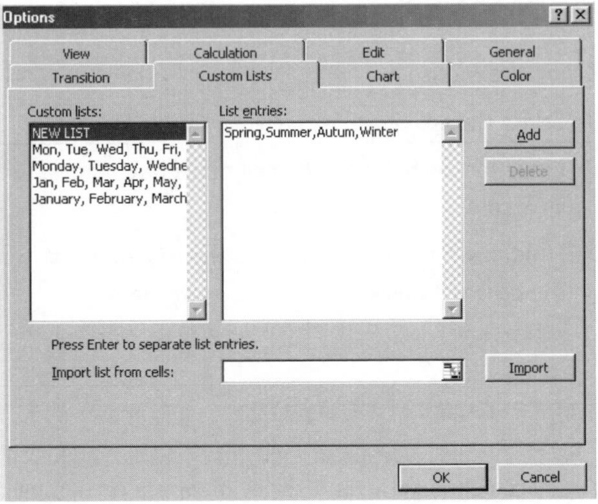

Figure 6.1

Creating a customised series.

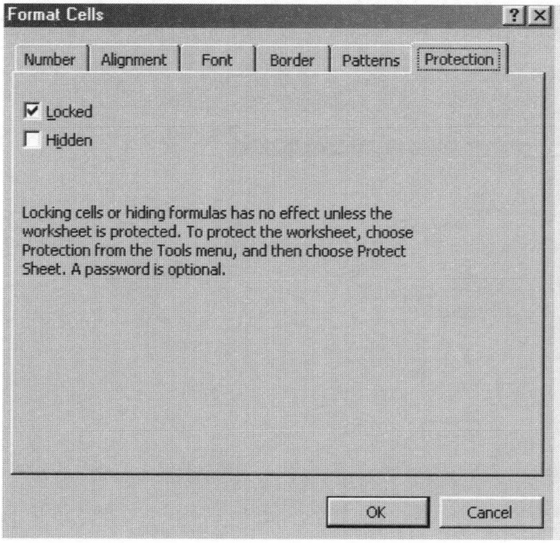

Figure 6.2

Tick the Locked check box to lock the cell.

Protecting cells

To avoid writing over a complex formula, you can protect your data:

1 Open the **Format** menu.

2 Select **Cells**.

3 Click the **Protection** tab.

The dialogue box warns you that locking cells or hiding formulas has no effect unless the worksheet is protected (Fig. 6.2).

To protect your worksheet:

1 Open the **Tools** menu.

2 Select **Protection**.

3 Choose **Protect Sheet** (Fig. 6.3).

4 Tick the boxes corresponding to the things you want to protect (Fig. 6.4).

5 If you want to, you can apply a password.

6 Click **OK**.

Figure 6.3

The Protect Sheet option in the Tools menu.

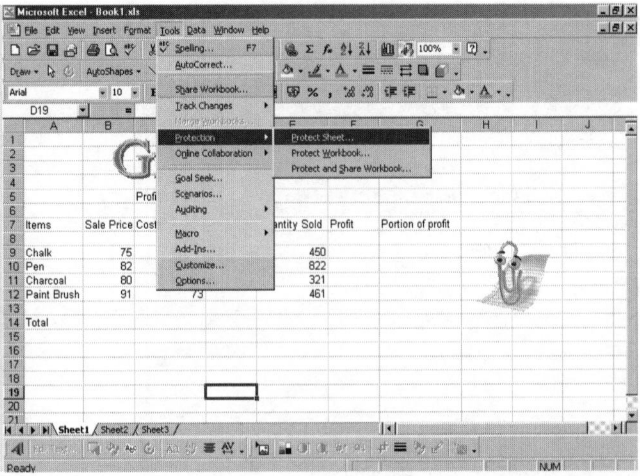

Figure 6.4

Protecting your worksheet.

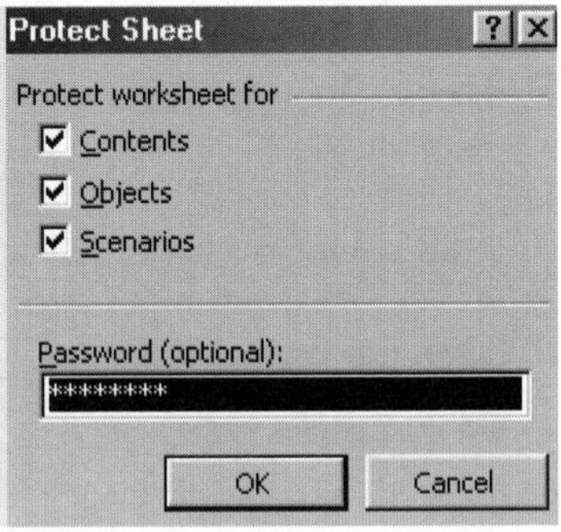

> If you lose or forget your password, you will have no way of recovering it. It is therefore advisable to keep a list of your passwords in a safe place. When typing passwords, remember that they are case sensitive.

All the cells in your worksheet are now write-protected. If you attempt to modify the contents of one of the cells, Excel displays the warning shown in Fig. 6.5.

Unprotect

To remove protection:

1 Open the **Tools** menu.

2 Select **Protection**.

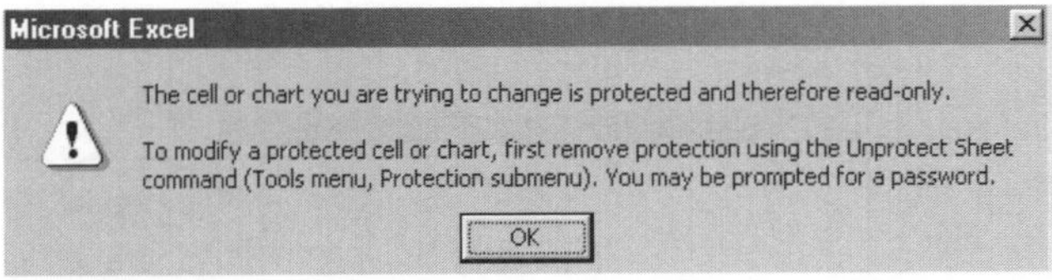

Microsoft Excel

! The cell or chart you are trying to change is protected and therefore read-only.

To modify a protected cell or chart, first remove protection using the Unprotect Sheet command (Tools menu, Protection submenu). You may be prompted for a password.

OK

Figure 6.5

Warning against modifying a locked cell.

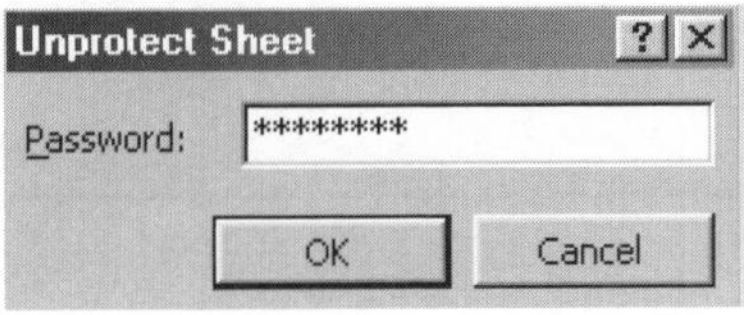

Unprotect Sheet

Password: ********

OK   Cancel

Figure 6.6

The Unprotect Sheet dialogue box.

3 Click **Unprotect Sheet**.

4 If you used a password, enter it in the box displayed (Fig. 6.6).

You can now rewrite in all the cells in your worksheet.

Naming a cell range

The usual row/column references are not always the best way to refer to cells.

Excel lets you give a name to a cell or a cell range. These names may be used instead of the references in all current operations.

Assigning a name

To name a cell or a range:

1 Select the cell(s) to be named.

2 Open the **Insert** menu.

3 Select **Name**.

4 Click **Define**.

5 Type in the name you want to give the cell(s) (Fig. 6.7).

6 Click **Add**.

7 Click **OK**.

Figure 6.7

Defining a name for a cell range.

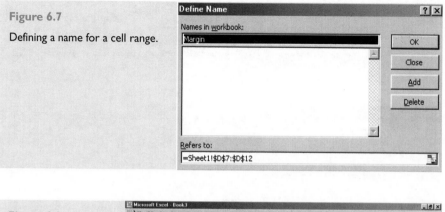

Figure 6.8

Executing an operation
using names.

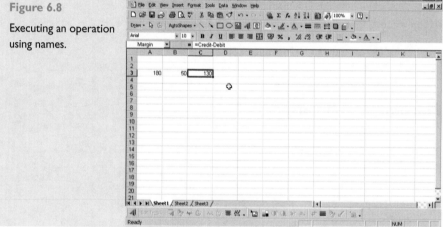

Using names

Once you have assigned a name to a cell or range, you can type in
the name of the cell(s) rather than the usual address.

For example, assume cell A3 contains the value 180 and is named
Credit, and cell B3 contains the value 50 and is named Debit. Cell C3
is named Sale, and will contain the result of A3-B3.

Instead of typing in =A3-B3, type in =Credit-Debit (Fig. 6.8).

Figure 6.9

The Go To function.

Displaying data

To find a named range of cells:

1 Open the **Edit** menu.

2 Select **Go To** option.

3 Choose the name you want to display from the list shown (Fig. 6.9).

4 Click **OK**.

Searching for data

To search for a particular word, phrase or figure in a worksheet:

1 Open the **Edit** menu.

2 Select **Find**.

3 Type in the text or number you wish to find (Fig. 6.10).

4 Click **Find Next**.

5 Once you have found what you are looking for, click **Close**.

Figure 6.10

The Find function.

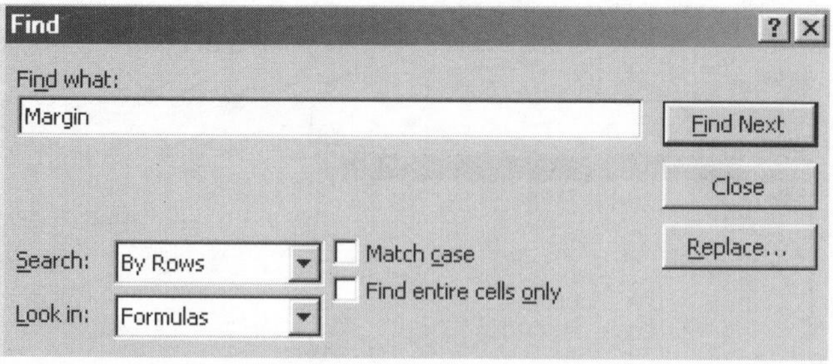

Figure 6.11

The Find and Replace function.

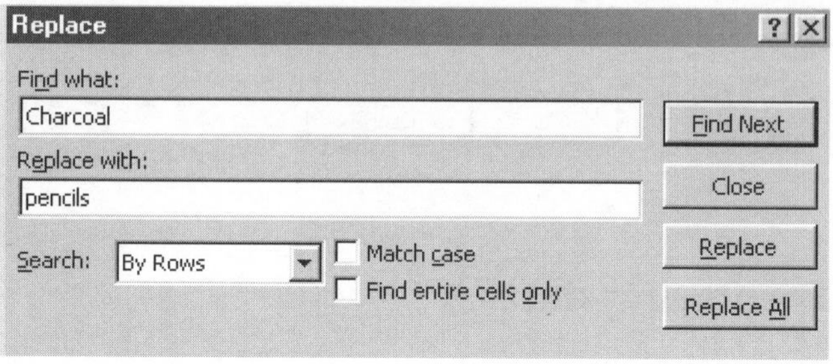

Replacing data

To replace a particular word, phrase or figure with another:

1 Open the **Edit** menu.

2 Select **Find**.

3 In the **Find What** box, type in the text or numbers you wish to replace.

4 Click the **Replace** button.

5 In the **Replace with** box, type in the text or numbers you want to replace the originals with (Fig. 6.11).

6 Click **Find Next** until you find the cells you are searching for.

7 Click **Replace** to enter the replacement text.

8 If you want to replace all occurencies of the original text/numbers, click on **Replace All** instead of **Find Next**.

The spell checker

To find and correct spelling errors:

1 Open the **Tools** menu.

2 Click **Spelling**.

You can also use the Spelling button (ABC) in the toolbar.

For each word that the spell checker does not recognise, you have a number of options:

● **Ignore**. Leaves the word as it is.

● **Change**. Corrects the word according to Excel's dictionary.

● **Add**. Adds the word to your custom dictionary – next time, Excel will assume that this word is spelled correctly.

● **Ignore All**. Ignores all further occurrences of the word.

● **Change All**. Corrects all occurrences of the word according to Excel's dictionary.

Sorting data

To sort data numerically, alphabetically or by logical values or empty cells:

1 Select the range to be sorted.

2 Open the **Data** menu.

3 Click **Sort**.

4 Choose your sorting methods in order of importance.

5 Click **OK**.

If you wish to sort data by alphabetical order, you can also select the range to be sorted then click on the **Sort Ascending** or **Sort Descending** button in the toolbar.

7

Advanced functions

- Creating an outline
- Using an outline
- Consolidating worksheets
- Modifying a consolidation
- Creating a PivotTable

Creating an outline

An outline allows you to apply a hierarchy to rows or columns. You use the same procedure as you would to divide a book into chapters and paragraphs.

Auto Outline

1 Select the sheet for which you wish to create an outline.
2 Open the **Data** menu.
3 Select **Group and Outline**.
4 Click **Auto Outline**.

Applying Auto Outline to the worksheet shown in Fig. 7.1 would produce the outline shown in Fig. 7.2.

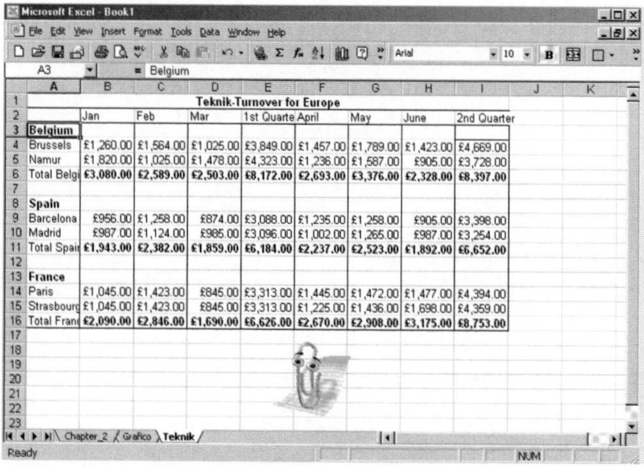

Figure 7.1

Example worksheet structure.

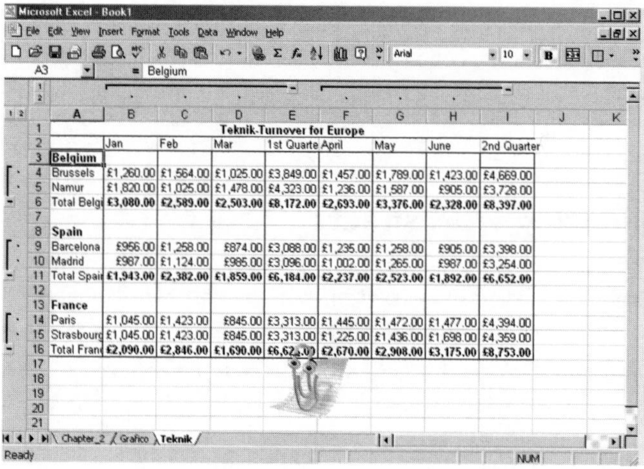

Figure 7.2

The same worksheet in outline.

Using an outline

If the outline symbols are not visible in the outline:

1 Open the **Tools** menu.

2 Select **Options**.

3 Click on the **View** tab.

4 Tick the **Outline symbols** box.

5 Click **OK**.

To decrease an outline so that it shows only the main hierarchies (in our example totals by country and by quarter), click the decrease (–) buttons in the left-hand and upper level bars. To re-show the lower hierarchies, click the increase (+) buttons.

Visible and invisible cells

If you copy cells from an outline worksheet that has been decreased to show only the main hierarchies, you will also copy only visible cells. To copy only visible cells:

1 Select the range you want to copy.

2 Open the **Edit** menu.

3 Click **Go To**.

4 Click **Special**.

5 Tick the Visible cells only box.

6 Click **OK**.

Consolidating worksheets

Excel lets you consolidate the data from two or more worksheets. For this example, we will use the tables shown in Fig. 7.3. Note that we have shown both tables on the same worksheet. You must create them in two separate worksheets, otherwise the procedure will not work.

1 Create two worksheets for the two tables shown in Fig. 7.3.

2 Open a new worksheet and name it.

3 Copy the non-variable elements from the two tables (in this case, the items and sale and cost prices) into the new worksheet.

4 Select the range in the new worksheet where you want to consoildate your data.

5 Open the **Data** menu.

6 Click on **Consolidate**.

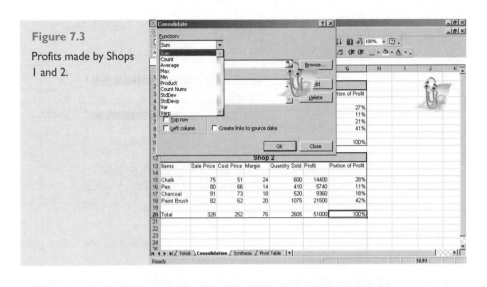

Figure 7.3

Profits made by Shops 1 and 2.

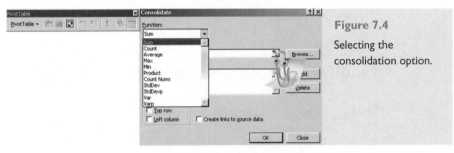

Figure 7.4

Selecting the consolidation option.

7 From the **Function** drop-down list, choose your consolidation option (Fig. 7.4). In our example, we choose Sum because we want to consolidate the profits for the two shops. Other options include Product and Average.

8 With the cursor in the **Reference** box, click on the tab for the first worksheet and select the cells to be consolidated (Fig. 7.5).

9 Click **Add**.

10 Select the tab for the next worksheet and select the cells to be consolidated.

11 Click **Add**.

Figure 7.5

Creating the references in the Consolidate dialogue box.

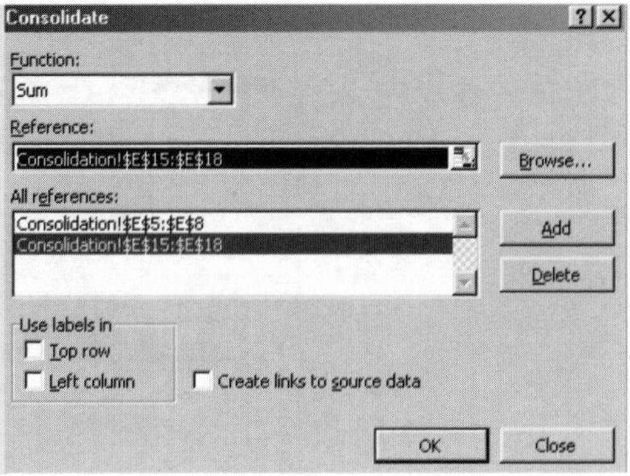

12 Repeat steps 10 and 11 until you have selected all the cells to be consolidated.

13 Click **OK**. The consolidated data should now be displayed in the new worksheet.

Modifying a consolidation

To change the type of consolidation used:

1 Select the range containing the consolidated data.

2 Open the **Data** menu.

3 Click on **Consolidate**.

4 In the **Function** box, select a different type of consolidation.

5 Click **OK**.

To remove a particular source's data from the consolidated values:

1 Select the range containing the consolidated data.

2 Open the **Data** menu.

3 Click on **Consolidate**.

4 Select the particular source in the **All references** box.

5 Click **Delete**.

6 Click **OK**.

To add another source's data to the consolidated values:

1 Select the range containing the consolidated data.

2 Open the **Data** menu.

3 Click on **Consolidate**.

4 With the cursor in the Reference box, click on the tab of the worksheet containing the data you want to add, and select the cells.

5 Click **Add**.

6 Click **OK**.

Creating a PivotTable

A PivotTable is a tool that lets you view the same table in different forms. It is a simple and effective method of displaying data in different ways for different end-users.

For example, we will take a class of five pupils studying three subjects (Fig. 7.6).

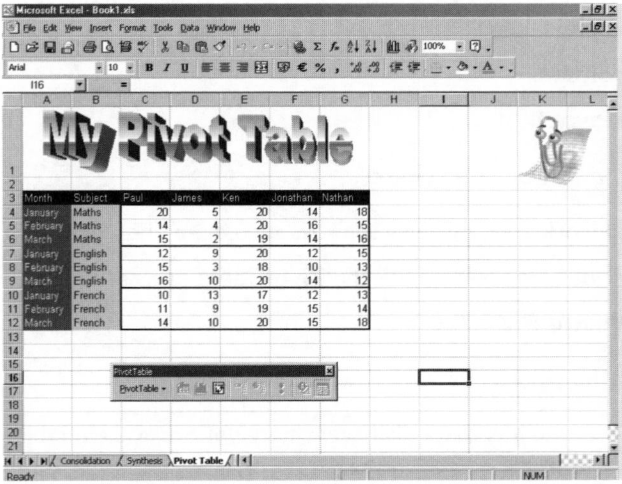

Figure 7.6

Starting data.

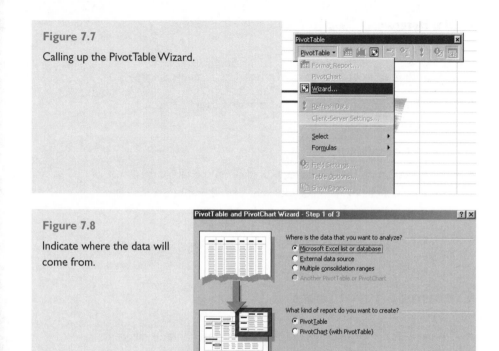

Figure 7.7

Calling up the PivotTable Wizard.

Figure 7.8

Indicate where the data will come from.

First of all, display the PivotTable toolbar:

1 Open the **View** menu.

2 Select **Toolbars**.

3 Click on **PivotTable**.

Now call up the PivotTable Wizard:

1 Select the work area, including the row and column headings.

2 On the PivotTable toolbar, click the **PivotTable** button.

3 Select **Wizard** (Fig. 7.7).

Now follow the wizard's instructions:

1 **Step 1.** Tick the box that tells Excel where your data are (in this case, **Microsoft Excel list or database**) (Fig. 7.8).

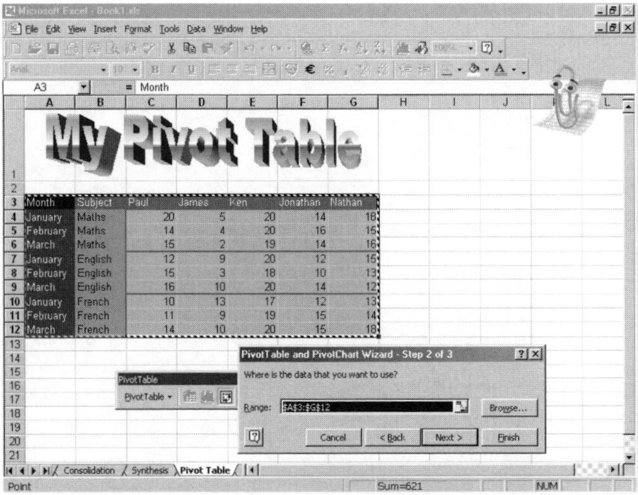

Figure 7.9
Selecting the data area.

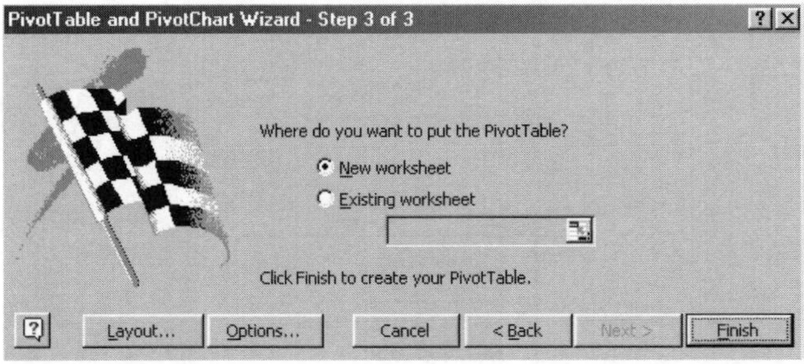

Figure 7.10
Displaying the results in a new worksheet.

2 **Step 2.** In the **Range** box, type in the area that defines your table (if you select the work area before calling up the wizard, as suggested above, the range will be defined automatically) (Fig. 7.9).

3 **Step 3.** Decide where you want to put the PivotTable (Fig. 7.10).

4 Still in the Step 3 dialogue box of the PivotTable Wizard, click the **Options** tab. In the **Format options** area, deselect all the formatting options (Fig. 7.11).

5 Click **OK**.

6 Back in the PivotTable Wizard dialogue box, select the **Layout** button.

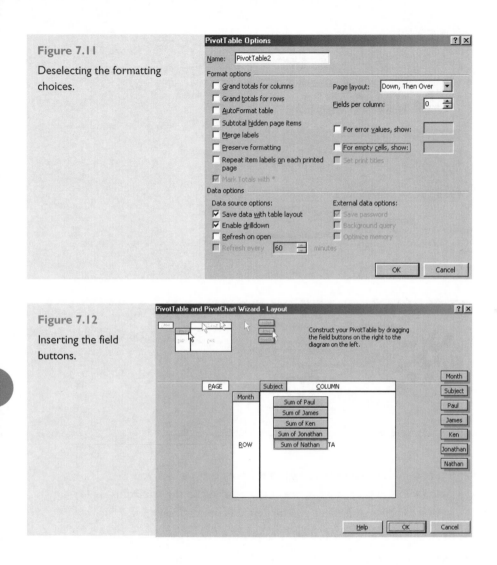

Figure 7.11

Deselecting the formatting choices.

Figure 7.12

Inserting the field buttons.

7 Drag the field buttons displayed on the right-hand side of the box that appears into the correct places in the diagram shown on the left (Fig.7.12).

8 Click **OK**.

9 Click **Finish**.

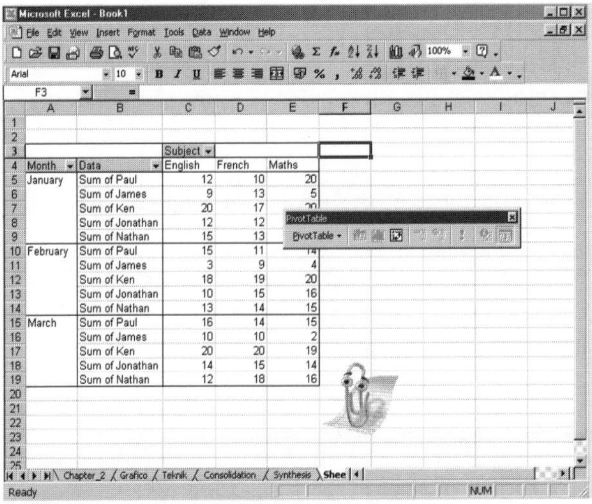

Figure 7.13

Your completed PivotTable.

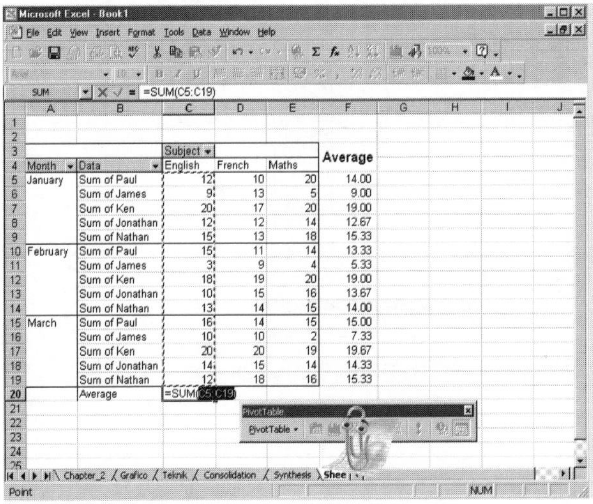

Figure 7.14

Creating two average columns.

Your PivotTable should now look something like that shown in Fig. 7.13.

But there are many other things you can do, apart from various displays, as you will see with the other work that we will be doing here. Create two Average records, as shown in Figure 7.14.

To customise your table:

1 Click on the drop-down arrow next to one of the column headings.

2 Tick (or un-tick) the data you do (or don't) want to show.

3 Click **OK**.

You can show all or just some of the data from each column at the same time.

Now create a column and a row of averages, as shown in Fig. 7.14. If you reduce the table (e.g. to show data for January only, Fig. 7.15), the averages will change with the table.

Figure 7.15

Averages displayed for a reduced table.

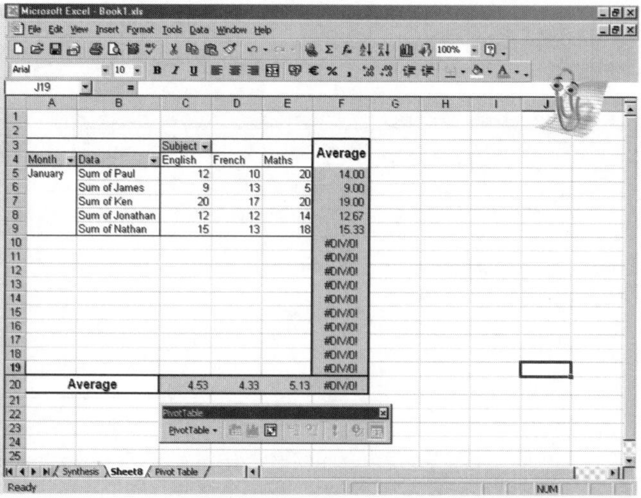

8

Creating a database

What is a database?

A database is a tool that allows you to manage, extract and filter information, then calculate and analyse data.

A database always starts with a first row that describes the file structure. Data must start immediately after the box name. Box names cannot contain punctuation signs or spaces.

For our example, we will use a database of five clients, their telephone numbers, and the last orders they requested (Fig. 8.1).

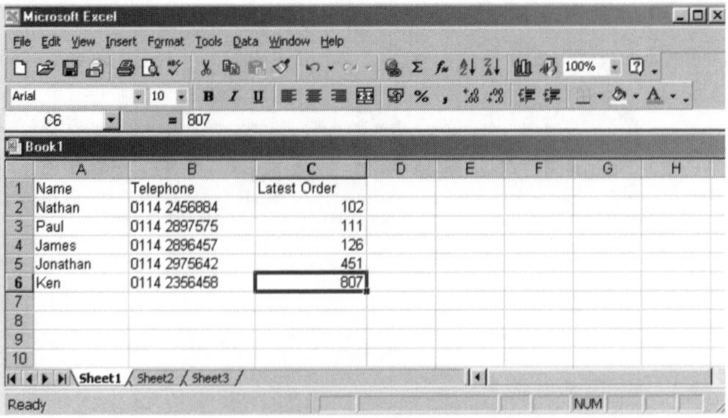

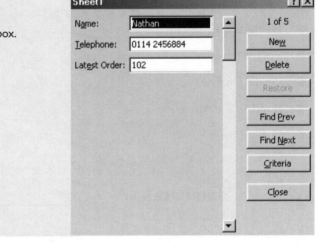

Figure 8.1

Our starting data.

Figure 8.2

The Entry form dialogue box.

Using the Entry form

This command displays a form in a dialogue box, which you can use to view, modify, add, delete and find entries in a database.
To see your database in the Entry form:

1 Select the table you have created.

2 Open the **Date** menu.

3 Click **Form**.

Move the scrollbar up or down to see each of your entries (Fig. 8.2).

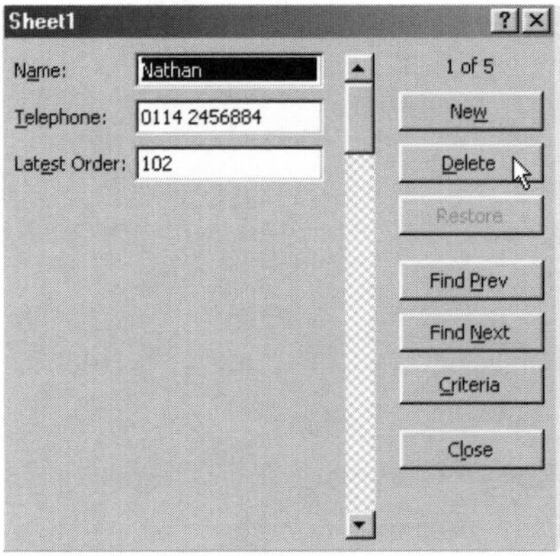

Figure 8.3

Deleting an entry.

Adding and deleting entries

To add an entry:

1   In the Entry form, click **New**.

2   Type in the new data.

3   Click **New** to confirm.

4   Press **Close**.

The new entry should now be displayed after the original data.
   To delete an entry:

1   In the Entry form, select the entry you wish to delete.

2   Click **Delete** (Fig. 8.3).

3   Confirm with **OK**.

4   Press **Close**.

Formatting

Excel provides numerous default formats to improve the look of
your database. You can also customise your own formats to change
the number of decimal places displayed and the currency symbol
used, among other things.

69

1 Open the **Format** menu.

2 Select **Cells**.

3 Click the **Number** tab.

In the drop-down **Category** list, you will find the following categories:

● **General**. General format cells have no specific number format. This is the default number format.

● **Number**. Used for general display of numbers. You can specify the number of decimal points, how negative numbers are displayed, and whether to use a separator in numbers over 999.

● **Currency**. Used for general monetary values. The Symbol list displays most international currency symbols.

● **Accounting**. Lines up the currency symbols and decimal points in a column. Again you can specify the currency symbol and number of decimal points.

● **Date**. Displays date and time serial numbers as date values. Use the Time format to display time only.

● **Time**. Displays date and time serial numbers as time values. Use the Date format to display date only.

● **Percentage**. Multiplies the cell value by 100 and displays the result with a % symbol.

● **Fraction**. Proposes fractions up to three digits.

● **Scientific**. Lets you specify the number of decimal points.

● **Text**. Cells are treated as text even when they contain a number. The cell is displayed exactly as entered.

● **Special**. Useful for tackling list and database values.

● **Custom**. Type the number format code, using one of the existing codes as a starting point.

Finding a file

To find a file, you can use Form or the database.
Find using Form:

1 Click anywhere in your database.

2 Open the **Data** menu.

3 Click **Form**.

4 Click **Criteria**.

5 Enter one or more conditions to find.

6 Click **Next** to confirm.

7 Click **Close**.

Your file is automatically displayed in full.
Find using the database:

1 Open the **Edit** menu.

2 Select **Find**.

3 In the **Find what** box, type in the text/numbers you are looking
   for (Fig. 8.4).

4 Click **Find Next**.

5 Once you've found what you want, click **Close**.

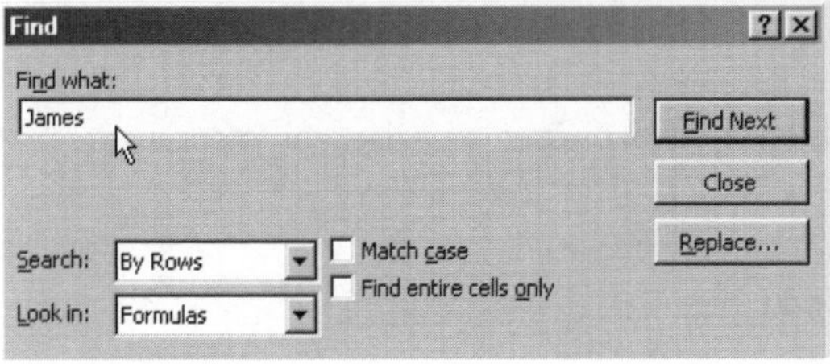

Figure 8.4

Finding using the database.

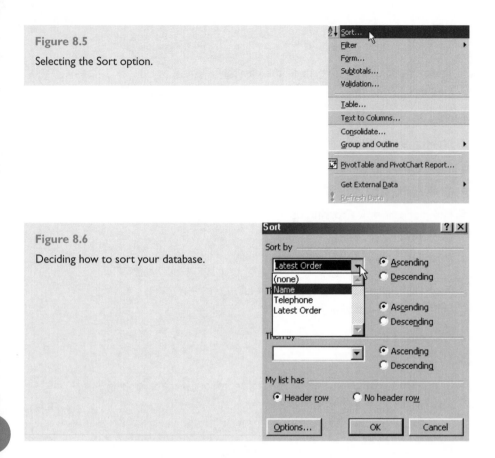

Figure 8.5

Selecting the Sort option.

Figure 8.6

Deciding how to sort your database.

Sorting a database

The Name field

You can sort your database according to alphabetical criteria.

1 Select your database.

2 Open the **Data** menu.

3 Select **Sort** (Fig. 8.5).

4 In the **Sort by** field, use the drop-down arrow to select how you want to sort your database (Fig. 8.6).

5 Click the **Ascending** or **Descending** button, depending on how you want the list to appear.

6 Click **OK**.

You can also apply Sort to a small selection rather than to the whole list. Simply select the area of the database you want to sort and proceed as before.

Using filters

AutoFilter

AutoFilter lets you display only certain parts of a database.

To activate AutoFilter:

1 Select your database.

2 Open the **Data** menu.

3 Select Filter.

4 Click on **AutoFilter**.

Your database should look something like that in Fig. 8.7.

To deactivate AutoFilter and restore the whole list, just repeat this procedure.

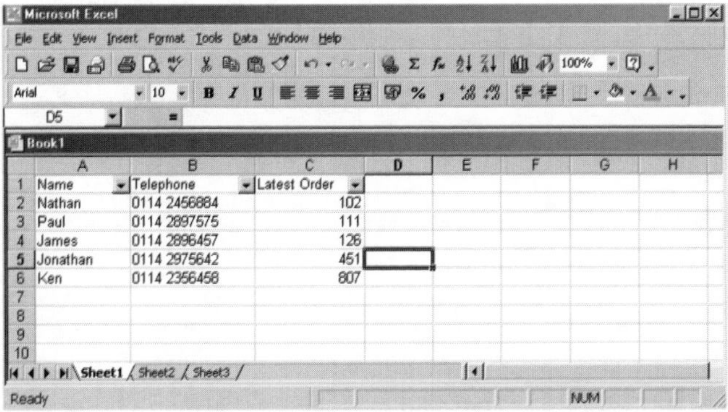

Figure 8.7

AutoFilter is active.

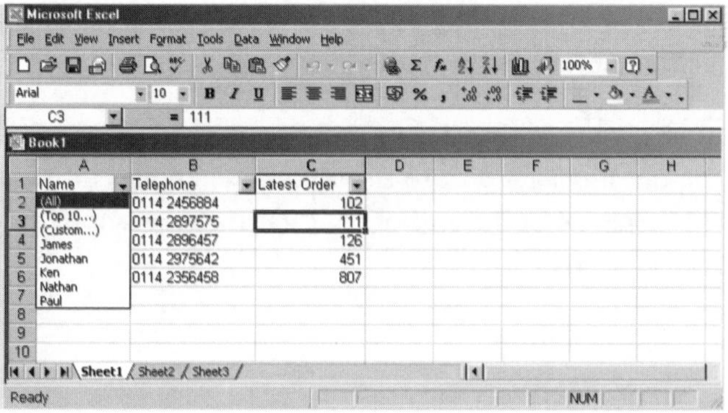

Figure 8.8

Using AutoFilter.

To filter the database, click on the drop-down arrow in one of the column headings and select the entry you are interested in (Fig. 8.8).

To redisplay the whole list:

1 Select the database.

2 Open the **Data** menu.

3 Select **Filter**.

4 Click **Show All**.

9

Creating a chart

- **Charts**
- **Getting started**
- **Changing the chart type**
- **Formatting a chart**

Charts

Chart production has become an integral part of the electronic office, just as much as text handling or accountancy packages. Charts are used in documents and accountancy reports to provide higher-impact messages.

To create a chart, you must first enter the data in a worksheet. Then you use the Chart Wizard to guide you through the process of creating a chart.

Which chart type do I choose?

There are six main chart types:

- **Line**. Used for indicating an evolving situation, e.g. sales for the first quarter.
- **Surface**. Shows trends in values across two dimensions in a continuous curve. Allows a good comparison of two different

values. Useful for highlighting the magnitude of an evolution, e.g. realised profit month by month for the last year.

- **Vertical bar**. Also called histograms or columns. Compares values across categories, e.g. variations over several years for employees, days off and salaries.

- **Pie**. Displays the contribution of each value to a total. Also used to show a split value, e.g. sales for a company split by geographical area.

- **Scatter**. Compares pairs of values, highlighting the cause–effect relationship, e.g. advertising costs and increase in sales.

- **Custom types**. Stock exchange, timescale pyramids, etc.

+info

A number of chart types can be combined. A single chart will plot multiple and different data, e.g. you could superimpose a histogram on a line chart to highlight the outcome of a specific series, or the best and worst sales results for the year. Be careful not to overload your charts with data: a surplus of data can cause the message to become blurred.

Getting started

For our example, we will use the data shown in Fig. 9.1. We want to chart ticket sales by month and destination.

Figure 9.1

The data before you create a chart.

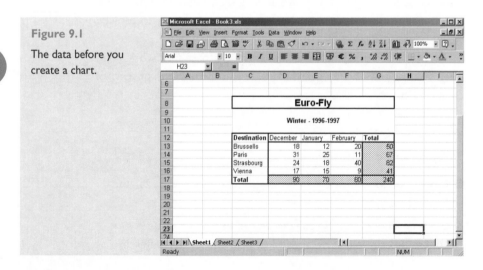

Destination	December	January	February	Total
Brussells	18	12	20	50
Paris	31	25	11	67
Strasbourg	24	18	40	82
Vienna	17	15	9	41
Total	90	70	80	240

Euro-Fly

Winter - 1996-1997

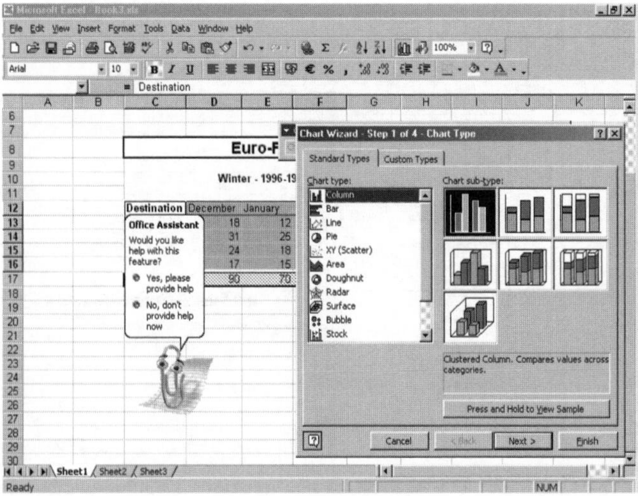

Figure 9.2
Choose the chart
type.

The best solution here is a histogram because we want to
compare values across categories.

To create the chart:

1 Select the data to be included in the chart.

2 Click the **Chart Wizard** icon in the Standard toolbar.

3 In the **Chart type** box, choose the sort of chart you want to
   create (in this case we will choose **Column**) (Fig. 9.2).

4 In the **Chart sub-type** area, click on the chart that you want
   to use.

5 Click **Next**.

6 In the next screen, select whether to display your series by rows
   or columns (in this case, click **Columns**, Fig. 9.3).

7 Click **Next**.

8 In the next dialogue box, click on the **Titles** tab, and give your
   chart a title in the **Chart title** box (Fig. 9.4).

9 The other tabs of this dialogue box let you add extra effects. Play
   about and see what happens.

10 Click **Next**.

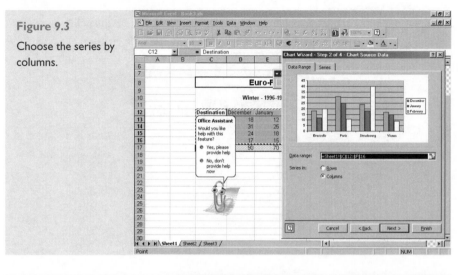

Figure 9.3

Choose the series by columns.

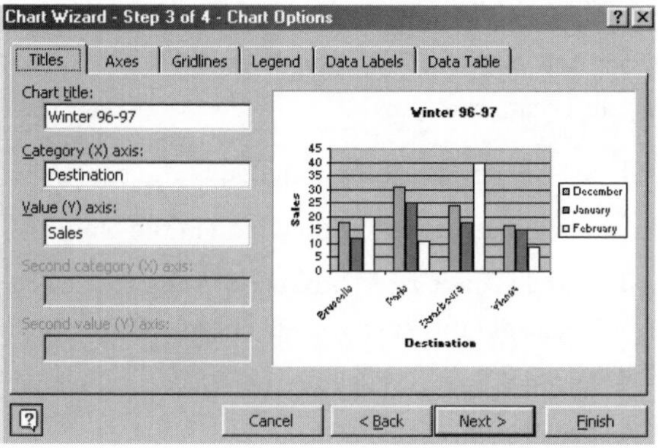

Figure 9.4

Give your chart a title.

11 In the final dialogue box, decide whether you want to create your chart as a new sheet or insert it into the existing worksheet (Fig. 9.5).

12 Click **Finish**.

Your chart is now placed in your worksheet. To move it to the right place, click anywhere in the chart and drag it to the required position. To change the size of the chart, click in the chart and drag the black resizing squares.

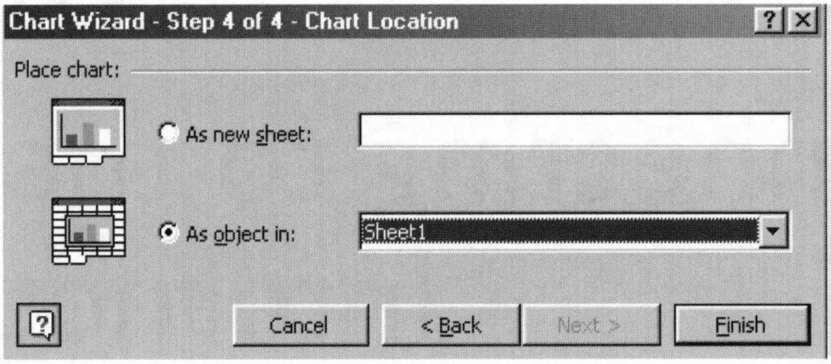

Figure 9.5
Selecting where to create your chart.

Changing the chart type

To change from one type of chart to another:

1 Click anywhere on the chart to activate it.

2 Click on the arrow in the **Chart Type** icon.

3 Choose the type of chart you would like to swap to.

Formatting a chart

To apply simple formatting to a chart:

1 Display the chart toolbar by clicking on **View, Toolbars, Chart**.

2 Click anywhere in your chart to activate it.

3 Select the **Format** icon in the Chart toolbar. (This icon changes its function (Format Chart Area, Format Plot Area, Format Chart Title) according to where you are in the chart when clicking on it.)

Avoid using red when formatting figures. This colour has a negative connotation. Use colours that match the company's corporate image and logo to create a coherent look for your charts.

4 From the Format dialogue box, choose your formatting in the usual way.

To format the title, click in the title to select it.

10

Connecting to the Internet

- Saving a document in **HTML** format
- Creating a hyperlink
- Inserting **URLs** in your worksheet

Excel 2000 lets you open your workbooks on the Internet. You can publish your own Web pages, view other files with hyperlinks, put your Excel files on the Internet, and search for new data to enhance your work.

To select the Web toolbar:

1 Open the **View** menu.

2 Select **Toolbars**.

3 Click **Web**.

Saving a document in **HTML** format

What is HTML?

HTML stands for Hypertext Markup Language. It is the file format used on the Web. HTML allows you to include sound files, images, video and templates on your sites.

An HTML file contains two categories of data:

- **Contents.** The information you want to display on your page, including text and images.

- **Tags.** These define the format and enhancements for the text. Tags are the invisible programming part of the page.

Saving in HTML format

1 Open the **File** menu.

2 Select **Save as Web Page** to bring up the Save As dialogue box (Fig. 10.1).

3 Click the **Publish** button.

4 In the **Item to Publish** box, use the drop-down arrow to select the worksheets or cells that you want to publish (Fig. 10.2).

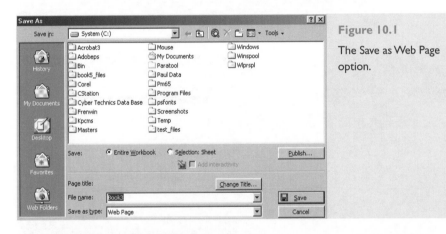

Figure 10.1

The Save as Web Page option.

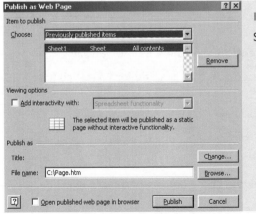

Figure 10.2

Selecting the data to be published.

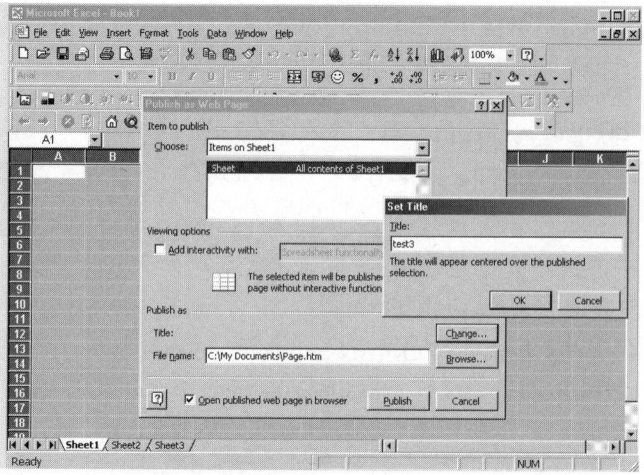

Figure 10.3

Giving your document a title.

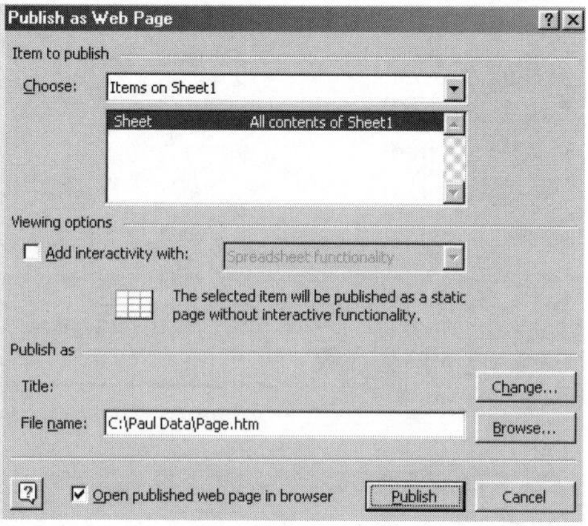

Figure 10.4

Specifying the address for your page.

5 In the **Publish as section**, click the **Change** button.

6 In the Set Title dialogue box, type in a title for your Web page (Fig. 10.3).

7 Confirm the title with **OK**.

8 In the **File name** box, type in the Internet address of your Web page (Fig. 10.4).

9 Click the **Publish** button at the bottom of the dialogue box.

Creating a hyperlink

A hyperlink links different types of data. It offers a shortcut to other workbooks and files.

Let us imagine that you wish to create a hyperlink in an Excel worksheet to a Word document.

1 Open the worksheet and the Word document you want to link.

2 Select the whole Word document.

3 Open the **Edit** menu and select **Copy**.

4 In the Excel spreadsheet, select the cell that will contain the hyperlink.

5 Open the **Edit** menu.

6 Select **Paste as Hyperlink** (Fig. 10.5).

> *To go from one workbook to another, simply click on a link (the address) which is automatically displayed in blue and underlined. When you have finished reading the file, the link changes from blue to mauve.*

The selected text is automatically displayed in the cell containing the link.

To activate the linked text, move the cursor over the link until it becomes a white hand (Fig. 10.6). Then click.

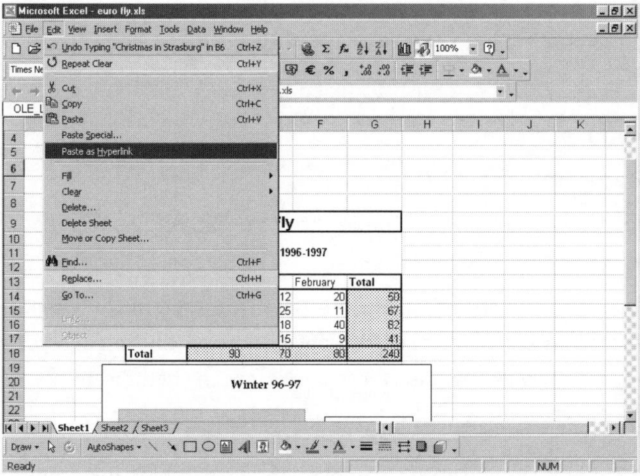

Figure 10.5

Select the Paste as Hyperlink option.

Figure 10.6

Click on the link when your
pointer becomes a small
white hand.

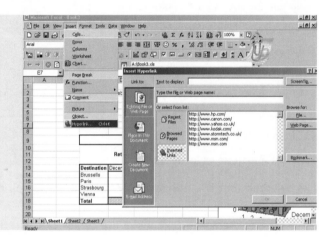

Figure 10.7

The Hyperlink option in
the Insert menu.

Inserting URLs in your worksheet

To create a hyperlink from your worksheet to a Web page:

1 Select the cell where you wish to place the hyperlink.

2 Open the **Insert** menu.

3 Select **Hyperlink** (Fig. 10.7).

4 In the **Text to display** box, type in the text that you want your
   link to appear as.

5 In the **Type the file or Web page name** box, type in the URL
   (uniform resource locator; the Web page address) of the page you
   are linking to, or click on one of the addresses in the box below.

6 Click **OK**.

To activate the link, move the cursor over the link until it becomes a
white hand, then click.

11

Printing your worksheet

- Using Print Preview
- Defining the print area
- Changing the page orientation
- Repeating titles on each page
- Centring the page
- Printing gridlines
- Printing in black and white
- Printing comments
- Printing a worksheet on several pages
- Printing several workbooks at the same time
- Printing a chart
- Printing a specific area in a worksheet
- Adding headers and footers
- Printing a worksheet
- Selecting a different printer

By default, clicking **Print** prints the whole worksheet in Excel's standard settings. There are various alternatives to these options.

Using Print Preview

To print your chart, start by previewing your worksheet to check it will look good when printed:

1 Open the **File** menu.

2 Select **Print Preview** (Fig. 11.1).

The print preview screen is now displayed with various buttons. To exit Print Preview, click on **Close**.

Zoom

Click on **Zoom** to magnify the Print Preview display. Click again to take the display back again.

Margins

If you click on the **Margins** button, you will activate the worksheet margins (Fig. 11.2). You can change the margins by dragging them left/right or up/down.

Figure 11.1

Selecting Print Preview.

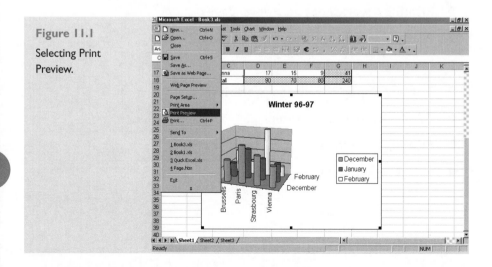

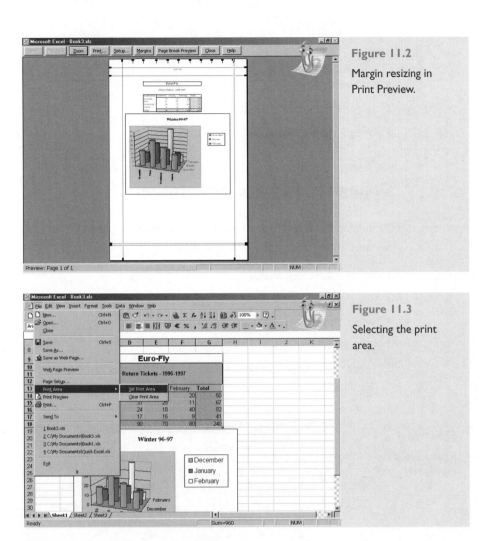

Figure 11.2

Margin resizing in Print Preview.

Figure 11.3

Selecting the print area.

Defining the print area

Say you want to print a worksheet without a chart that you created:

1 Select the bit of the worksheet that you want to print.

2 Open the **File** menu.

3 Select **Print Area**.

4 Click **Set Print Area** (Fig. 11.3).

If you now send to print, only the selected area will be printed.
To deselect your print area:

1 Open the **File** menu.

2 Select **Print Area**.

3 Click **Clear Print Area**.

Changing the page orientation

By default, Excel will print your worksheet with a portrait (vertical) orientation. To change to landscape (horizontal) orientation:

1 Select your work area.

2 Open the **File** menu.

3 Select **Page Setup**.

4 Click the **Page** tab.

5 Select the **Landscape** radio button in the Orientation section (Fig. 11.4).

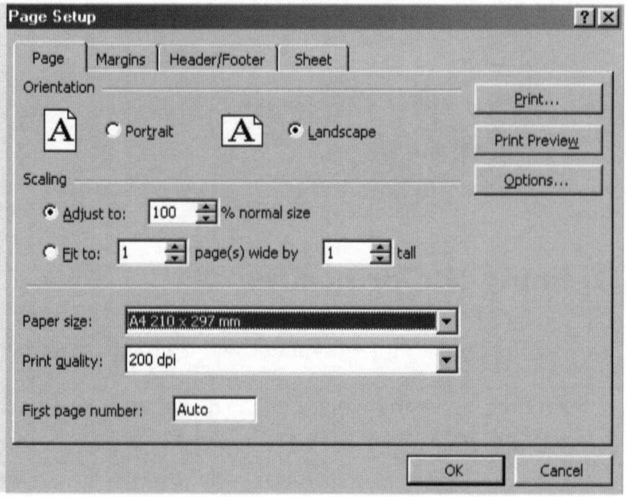

Figure 11.4

Selecting landscape orientation.

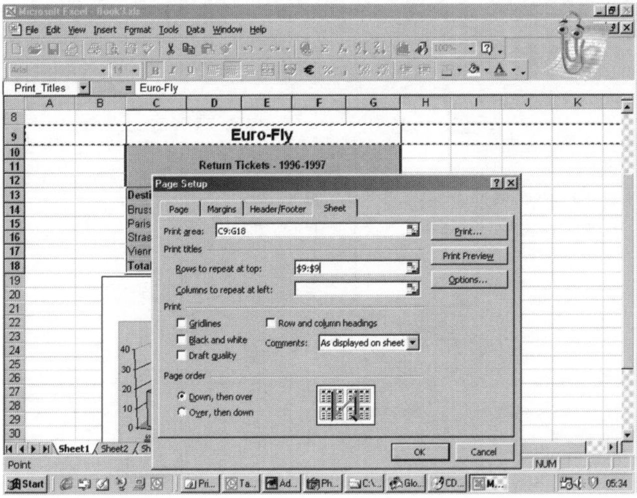

Figure 11.5

Selecting row titles to appear on each page.

Repeating titles on each page

If you have column or row titles, you may wish them to be printed on each page in your worksheet.

1 Open the **File** menu.

2 Select **Page Setup**.

3 Click the **Sheet** tab (Fig. 11.5).

4 In the **Print titles** text area, specify the row/column titles you want to be displayed on all the pages.

Centring the page

To centre your work area on the page:

1 Go to **File**, Page **Setup**.

2 Click the **Margins** tab (Fig. 11.6).

3 In the **Center on page** section, tick the **Horizontally** and **Vertically** boxes.

4 Click **OK**.

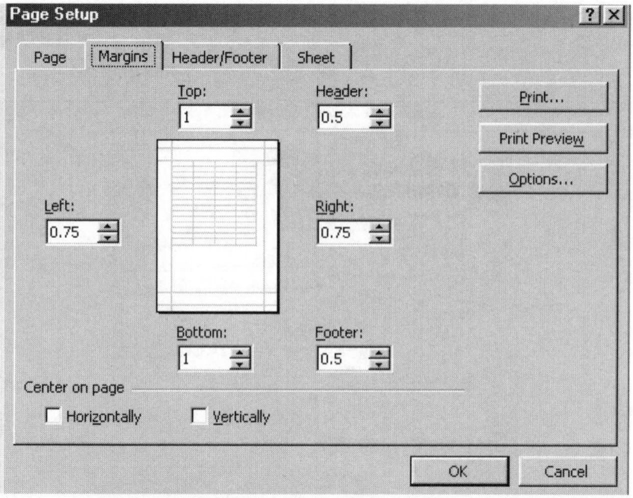

Figure 11.6
Defining the margins.

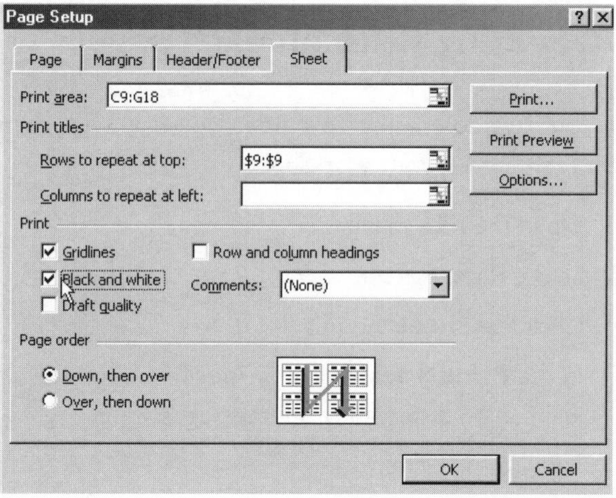

Figure 11.7
Printing gridlines.

Printing gridlines

1 Open the **File** menu.

2 Select **Page Setup**.

3 Click the **Sheet** tab (Fig. 11.7).

4 In the **Print** section, tick the **Gridlines** box.

Printing in black and white

If you have formatted data with colour but you only have a black and white printer:

1 Open the **File** menu.

2 Select **Page Setup**.

3 Click the **Sheet** tab.

4 In the **Print** section, tick the **Black and white** box.

If you tell a black and white printer to print a colour document, it will print in grayscale. To reduce printing time, make sure you tick the Black and White check box.

Printing comments

If you wish to print your worksheet with comments at the end:

1 Open the **File** menu.

2 Select **Page Setup**.

3 Click the **Sheet** tab.

4 In the **Comments** drop-down box, select **At end of sheet**.

If you want to print comments as they are displayed in your worksheet:

1 Open the **File** menu.

2 Select **Page Setup**.

3 Click the **Sheet** tab.

4 In the **Comments** drop-down box, select **As displayed on sheet** (Fig. 11.8).

Printing a worksheet on several pages

To print your worksheet on several pages:

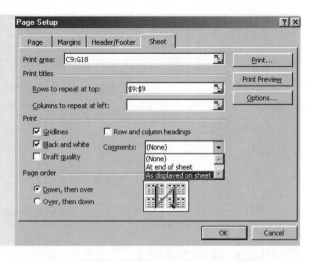

Figure 11.8

Choosing to display comments.

Figure 11.9

Ticking the Fit to box.

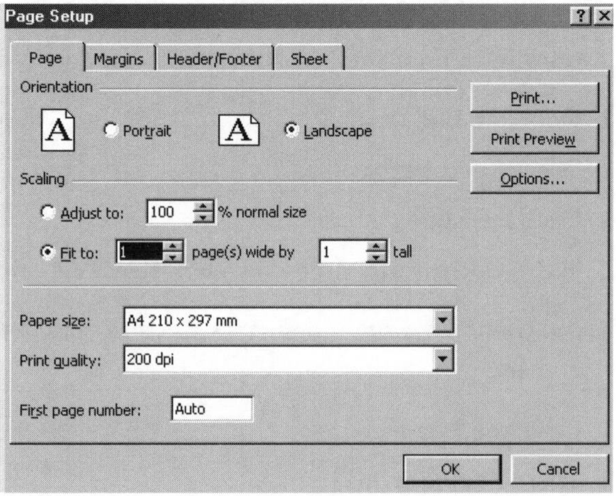

1 Open the **File** menu.

2 Select **Page Setup**.

3 Click the **Page** tab.

4 Tick the **Fit to** box (Fig. 11.9).

5 Specify, in numbers of pages, the width and height for your print-out.

6 Click **OK**.

Printing several workbooks at the same time

You can print several workbooks if they are all in the same directory:

1 Open the **File** menu.

2 Select **Open**.

3 Keep the **Ctrl** key pressed while you click all the workbooks you wish to print.

4 Click the **Tools** button.

5 Select **Print**.

Printing a chart

To print a chart but not the worksheet it is contained within:

1 Select the chart.

2 Open the **File** menu.

3 Choose **Page Setup**.

4 Click the **Chart** tab.

5 In the **Printed chart size** section, choose the required size option.

6 Click **Print**.

Printing a specific area in a worksheet

To print a specific area in a worksheet:

1 Open the **View** menu.

2 Select **Page Break Preview** (Fig. 11.10).

3 In this view, select the area you want to print.

Figure 11.10

Selecting Page Break
Preview.

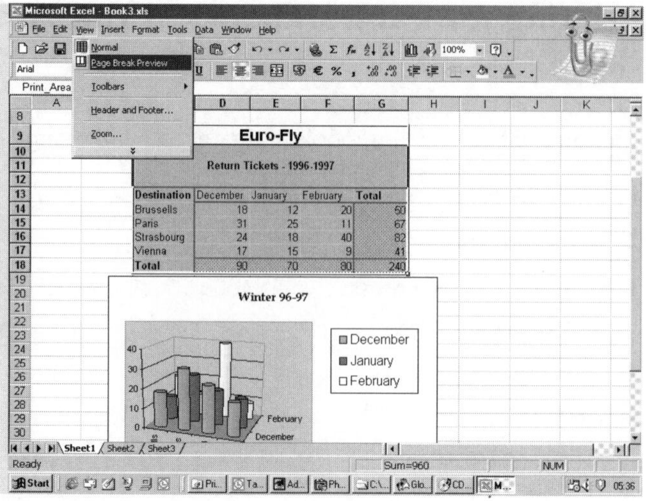

4 Click with the right mouse button in the selected area.

5 Select **Set Print Area** from the context menu.

6 Now print.

Adding headers and footers

Before printing, you can add a header and a footer that will appear on every page. You can select predefined templates or create your own.

A worksheet can have only one header and one footer. Adding a new header will replace the original header.

Custom headers and footers

To customise your own headers and footers:

1 Open the **View** menu.

2 Select **Header and Footer**.

3 Click the **Custom Header** button.

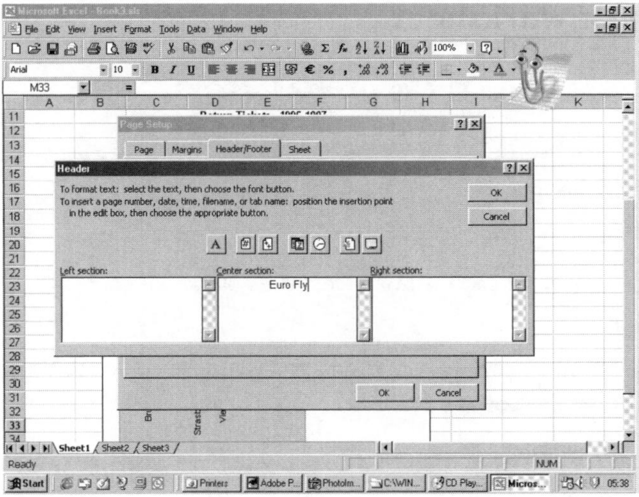

Figure 11.11
Customising your headers and footers.

4 Create your header by typing the header text into the **Left section**, **Center section** and **Right section** boxes to left-align, centre or right-align your text (Fig. 11.11).

5 Use the **Font** button to format the text.

6 Use the **Page Number**, **Total Pages**, **Date**, **Time**, **File Name** and **Sheet Name** buttons to automatically add extra information.

7 Click **OK**.

8 If you also want to add a custom footer, click on the **Custom Footer** button.

9 When you have finished, click **OK**.

Default headers and footers

To add default headers and footers:

1 Open the **View** menu.

2 Select **Header and Footer**.

3 In the **Header and Footer** drop-down boxes, select the ones you want to apply.

4 Click **OK**.

Printing a worksheet

Once you have established all the settings, you can print your worksheet:

1 Open the **File** menu.

2 Select **Print**.

3 In the **Number of copies** box, select the number of copies you wish to print.

4 If you are printing several copies, and you want the copies to be collated, tick the **Collate** box.

5 Confirm by clicking **OK**.

Selecting a different printer

If you use several printers with your computer, you can choose the one to print your worksheet on:

1 Open the **File** menu.

2 Select **Print**.

3 In the **Printer** area, select the printer from the drop-down box.

4 Confirm by clicking **OK**.

appendix
Excel and the euro

The euro currency symbol

O n 1 January 2002, the euro will become the sole currency for 11 countries in the EU. To change the default currency your PC uses to the euro:

1 On the Windows desktop, click on **My Computer**, **Control Panel**, **Regional Settings**. Click on the Currency tab (Fig. A.1).

2 In the **Currency symbol** box, select the euro symbol.

3 Click **Apply**, then **OK**.

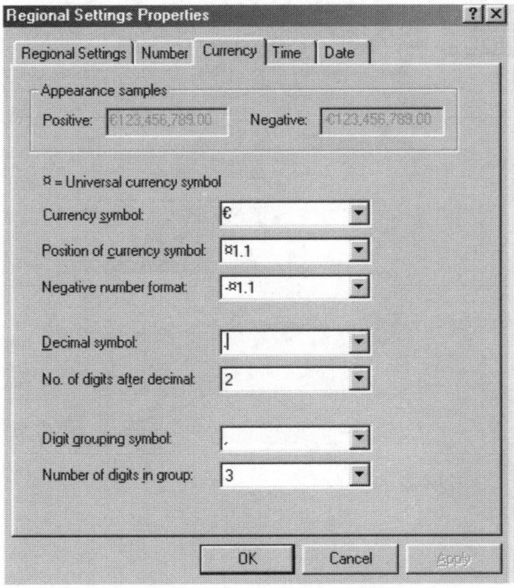

Figure A.1

This is where you default currency symbol in Windows.

Once the euro has been defined in Regional Settings, it is automatically included in all Windows applications.

The euro in Excel

If you are only going to use the euro in Excel:

1 Select the worksheet or the range of cells where you need to use the euro sign.

2 Click inside the selection with the right mouse button and select **Format Cells**.

3 Select the **Number** tab (Fig. A.2).

4 In the **Category** list, select **Currency**.

5 In the **Symbol** list, select the euro symbol.

6 Click **OK**.

The values in the selected range of cells should now be expressed as euros (Fig. A.3).

Figure A.2

Selecting the euro symbol.

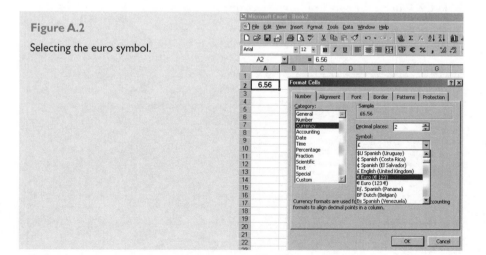

Currency conversion

Excel 2000 comes with an add-in program that provides tools to work with euros and to convert the national currencies of the countries in the euro area.

Loading the Euro Currency Tools

The Euro Currency Tools are not loaded with Excel 2000. They are add-in programs that can be downloaded from the Microsoft Web site. To do this:

1 Insert the CD for Office 2000 or Excel 2000 into your CD-ROM drive.

2 Click **Tools, Add-Ins**. In the dialogue box displayed, tick the **Euro Currency Tools** check box (Fig. A.4).

3 Click **OK**.

The formatting toolbar now contains the Euro button (Fig. A.5), and the EUROCONVERT worksheet function is now available.

Figure A.4

Installing Euro Currency Tools.

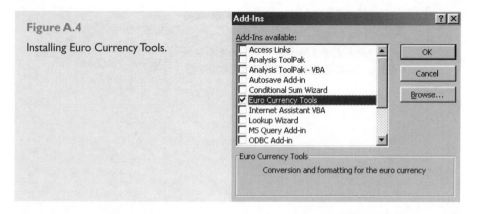

Figure A.5

The Euro button on the formatting toolbar.

Using Euro Currency Tools

Use the Euro button to apply the euro currency style. It assumes that you are working in euro values. If you are not working in euro values, then you need to use the EUROCONVERT function.

Table A.1 Codes for Euro countries' currencies.

Country	Currency	ISO Code
Austria	Schilling	ATS
Belgium	Franc	BEF
Finland	Markka	FIM
France	Franc	FRF
Germany	Deutschmark	DEM
Ireland	Punt	IEP
Italy	Lira	ITL
Luxembourg	Franc	LUF
Netherlands	Guilder	NLG
Portugal	Escudo	PTE
Spain	Peseta	ESP
Euro member states	Euro	EUR

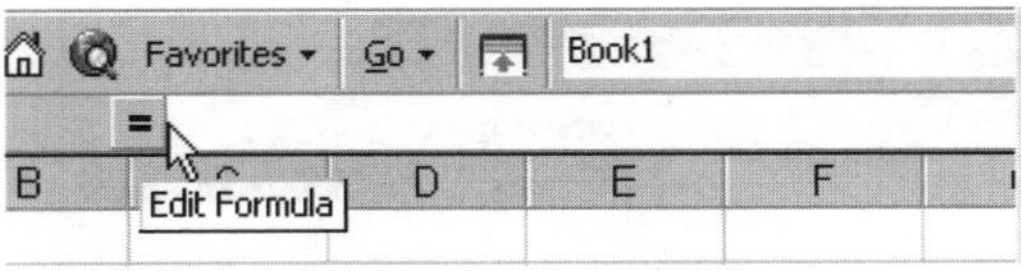

Figure A.6

The Edit Formula button.

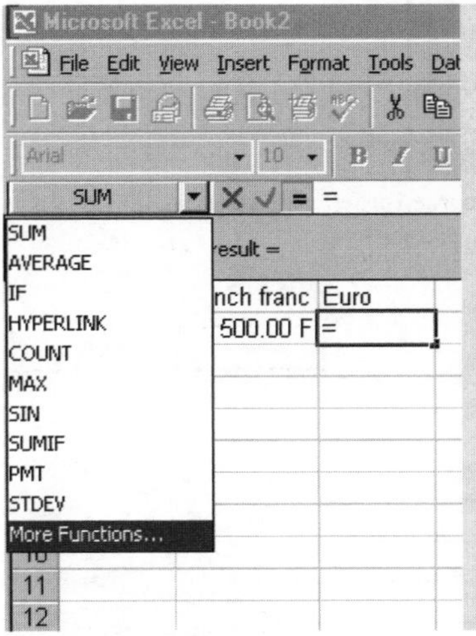

Figure A.7

The functions available.

To use the EUROCONVERT function:

1 Click the cell that will contain the result of the conversion.

2 Click the **Edit Formula** button at the top of the screen (Fig. A.6).

3 Click the list on the left-hand side of the Formula bar to get a choice of functions.

4 Select **More Functions** from the drop-down list (Fig. A.7).

5 In the dialogue box displayed, select **User Defined** (Fig. A.8).

6 Select **EUROCONVERT**.

7 Click **OK**.

8 In the **Number** box, type in the value you want to convert, or the cell reference (Fig. A.9).

9 In the **Source** box, type in the three-letter code for the currency that you are converting from (Table A.1).

Figure A.8
Finding EUROCONVERT.

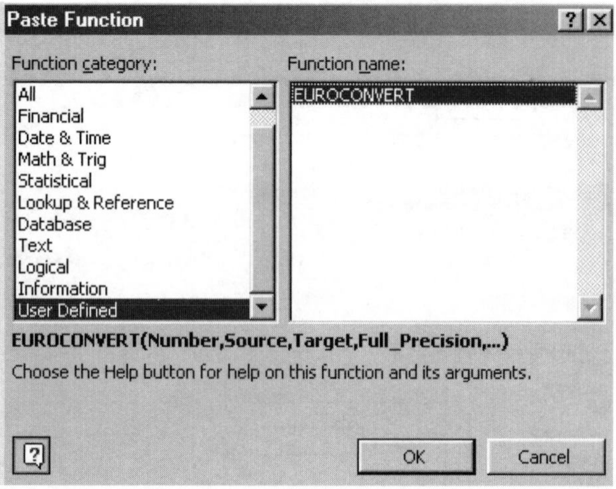

Figure A.9
EUROCONVERT has all the required calculation elements.

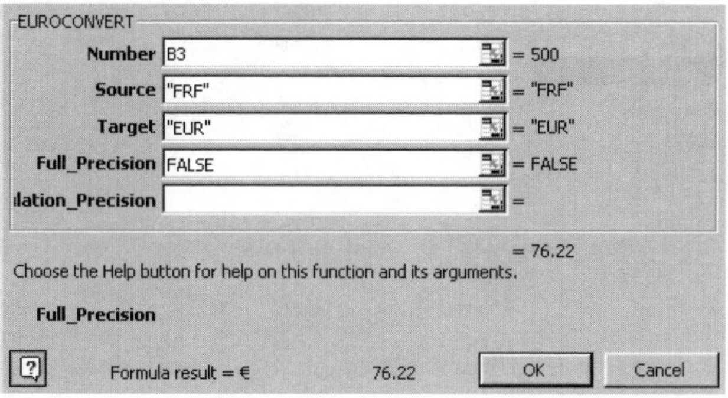

10 In the **Target** box, type in the three-letter code for the currency you are converting to.

11 In the **Full-Precision** box, type in **TRUE** to use a six-digit conversion factor, or **FALSE** to use a currency-specific conversion factor.

12 Click **OK**.

index